Singing the Clay:

Pueblo Pottery of the Southwest

Yesterday and Today

Bill Mercer

Cincinnati Art Museum

AF798410

Exhibition Presenter:
The Lois and Richard Rosenthal Foundation
This catalogue is funded in part by the August A. Rendings, Jr. Foundation,
W. Roger Fry, Trustee

Published in conjunction with the exhibition:
SINGING THE CLAY:
PUEBLO POTTERY OF THE SOUTHWEST,
YESTERDAY AND TODAY

Exhibition Schedule

Cincinnati Art Museum
Cincinnati, Ohio
February 12, 1995, to June 4, 1995

Chrysler Museum
Norfolk, Virginia
October 14, 1995, to January 7, 1996

Fort Wayne Museum of Art
Fort Wayne, Indiana
September 6, 1997, to November 2, 1997

Exhibition presenter of
Singing the Clay:
Pueblo Pottery from the Southwest,
Yesterday and Today:
The Lois and Richard Rosenthal Foundation
This catalogue is funded in part by the
August A. Rendings, Jr. Foundation, W. Roger Fry, Trustee.

Copyright © 1995
by the Cincinnati Art Museum
All rights reserved.
No part of this publication may be reproduced in any manner whatsoever
without permission in writing from the Cincinnati Art Museum.

Library of Congress Cataloging-in-Publication Data
Mercer, Bill, 1960-
Singing the Clay: Pueblo pottery of the Southwest, yesterday and today/ Bill Mercer
p. cm.
Catalog of an exhibition held at the Cincinnati Art Museum Feb. 12, 1995-June 4, 1995.
ISBN 0-931537-18-5 (pbk. : acid-free paper)
1. Pueblo pottery—Themes, motives—Exhibition. 2. Pueblo pottery—Classification—Exhibitions. 3. Pueblo Indians—Antiquities—Exhibitions. 4. Cincinnati Art Museum—Exhibitions.
I. Cincinnati Art Museum. II. title.
E99.P9M42 1995
738.3'089'974079—dc20 95-5191
CIP

Designed by Deborah Leffert

Edited by Ann Cotter

Printed and bound in U.S.A.

Jacket illustration:
Front cover: Zia Polychrome Jar, ca. 1950
Back cover: Zia Polychrome Jar, 1994

FOREWORD

Extraordinary efforts are being made today to preserve and carry on Native American cultural traditions. These efforts have important implications for museum practice. *Singing the Clay: Pueblo Pottery of the Southwest, Yesterday and Today* respects the dual need to honor artistic achievements of the past and to demonstrate the continuity and vitality of contemporary artistic expressions. We are especially pleased that the exhibition has afforded the opportunity to add a major group of objects by contemporary Pueblo Indian artists to the Cincinnati Art Museum's outstanding historic collection. Thanks are due to the CAM's Bill Mercer for his sensitive selection and informed interpretation of this wonderful exhibition. We also acknowledge with gratitude The Lois and Richard Rosenthal Foundation and other generous donors without whose support this project would not have been possible.

Barbara K. Gibbs
Director

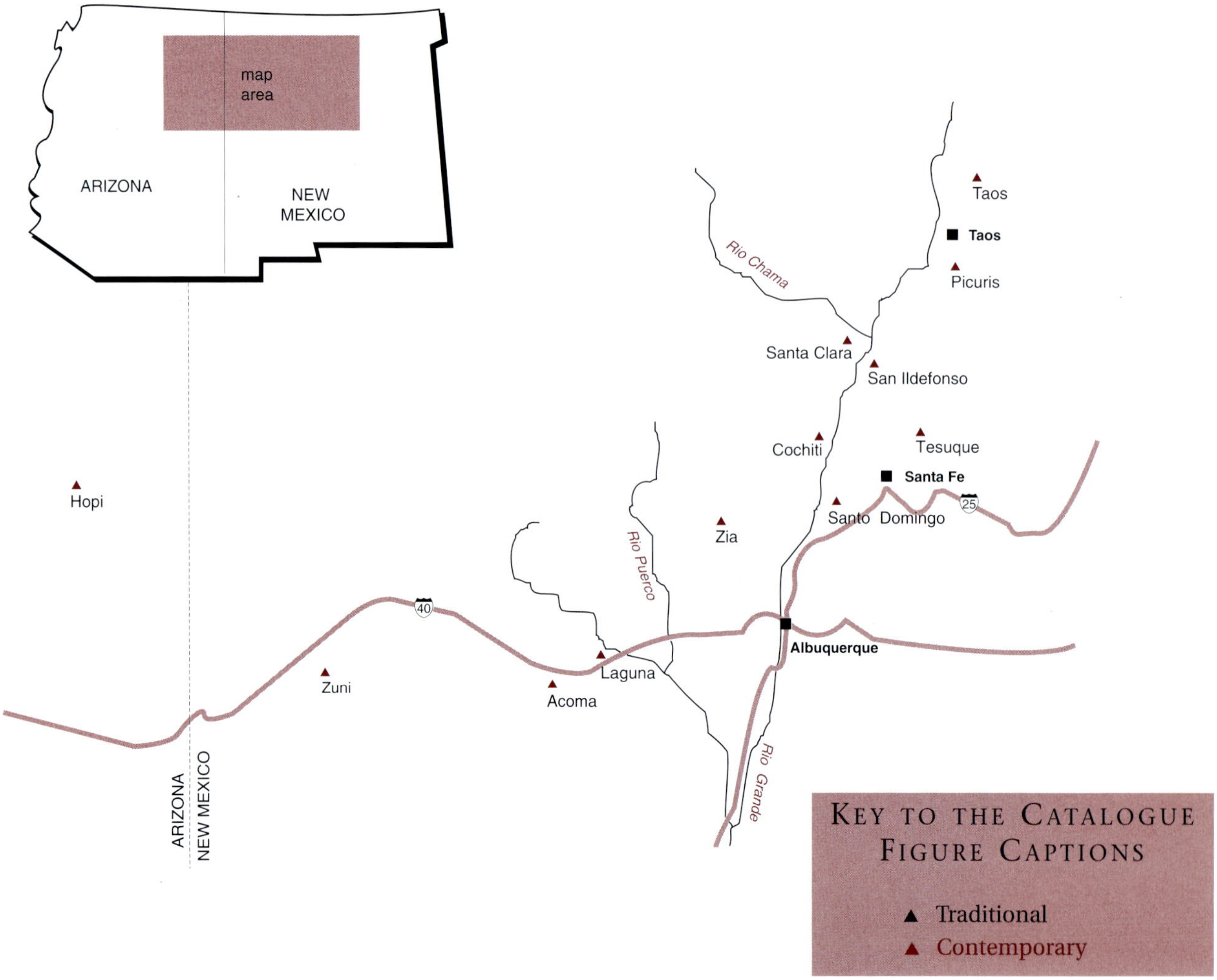

▲ *Pueblos represented in the exhibition are illustrated on the map.*

Introduction
History of the CAM Collection

The Cincinnati Art Museum has a long history of collecting Native American objects, especially Pueblo pottery, being one of the first art museums in the United States to acquire and exhibit these objects as art. Among the first items incorporated into the Museum's collection, in 1881, was Native American pottery. Currently the Museum's collection includes more than 300 examples of Pueblo pottery, illustrating a full range of styles and techniques, and is one of the strongest areas of the Native American collection. While the Museum has collected Native American art objects throughout its history, most of the Pueblo pottery came to it through a series of four unrelated acquisitions.

The Museum's first major acquisition of Pueblo pottery came in 1885, an exchange between the Cincinnati Art Museum Association and the National Museum of Natural History, Smithsonian Institution. The Museum sent the Smithsonian examples of Rookwood pottery in exchange for Native American objects that were considered to be duplicates, including thirty-one pieces of pottery from Hopi, Zuni, Acoma and Santa Clara pueblos collected in the late 1870s and early 1880s by James Stevenson, John Wesley Powell, and Cosmos and Victor Mindeleff under the auspices of the Bureau of American Ethology.

The second large group of Pueblo pottery to be acquired by the Museum came the following year. In 1886 the Denver and Rio Grande Western Railroad, commonly known as the "Chili Line," which extended southward as far as Espanola, New Mexico, donated eighty-two vessels. Among the micaceous vessels are human figures (figs. 74-76) and small eccentric shapes such as lizards, deer, cats, and melons. In addition, the gift also includes a number of miniature bowls decorated with loosely painted designs on a gray slip. Virtually all of these examples are identified as having been made at Tesuque Pueblo and are indicative of the small pieces made in the 1880s for the emerging Native American arts and crafts market.

Another major addition to the Native American collection came to the Museum as the gift of Amelia Elizabeth White. In 1937, as she was closing her Gallery of American Indian Art in New York City, White dispersed the remaining inventory to several institutions, including the Cincinnati Art Museum. The material was primarily from the Plains and Southwest regions, most notably a series of watercolors by Pueblo artists such as Alfonso Royba (Awa Tsireh) and Tonita Pena (Quah Ah), but also included twenty-three pottery vessels highlighted by a large Zuni drum (fig. 94), Santo Domingo dough bowls (figs. 58, 59), and a large Santa Clara storage jar (fig. 47). After closing her New York shop, White moved to Santa Fe, New Mexico, and became involved with the Indian Arts Fund and eventually donated the property where the School of American Research is now located.

The latest major addition of Pueblo pottery to the Museum's collection has occurred in support of the exhibition, "Singing the Clay: Pueblo Pottery of the Southwest, Yesterday and Today." One of the purposes of the exhibition is to focus attention on contemporary Pueblo pottery that continues to be created in the traditional manner. Therefore, in 1994, the Museum acquired a total of thirty-eight vessels in order to illustrate the continuity of traditional styles and techniques from those Pueblos already represented the collection; Hopi, Zuni, Acoma, Laguna, Zia, Santo Domingo, Tesuque, San Ildefonso, Santa Clara, Taos, and Picuris. At each Pueblo the Museum obtained three or four vessels from at least two different families. The majority of the vessels were commissioned and purchased directly from the artists for the Museum by Bill Mercer, assistant curator for the Art of Africa and the Americas, in consultation with Mary Lewis Garcia, a daughter of Lucy Lewis, who is herself a traditional potter from Acoma Pueblo.

The People, The Pottery

There are about twenty Pueblo Indian groups today with a total population of about 50,000. While they are modern people, Pueblo Indians also successfully continue with their own established social values, religious institutions, and artistic traditions. One of the most enduring Pueblo artistic traditions is the creation of beautiful pottery vessels that provide both a link to the past and a symbol of a dynamic future.

Their homeland, and that of their ancestors, is the southwestern part of the United States, including what is now New Mexico, Arizona, and parts of Colorado and Utah. Most tribal members live in their villages, called pueblos, which are situated along the Rio Grande River and its tributaries from Taos to south of Albuquerque, New Mexico; westward to the pueblos of Acoma, Laguna, and Zuni; and even further west to the Hopi villages located in northeastern Arizona. It is an arid region, noted for high plateaus and punctuated by rugged mountain ranges and spectacular landscapes, where rainfall can be less than ten inches per year. Although blessed with a great variety of natural resources, this fragile environment is also subject to the potentially damaging forces of nature, such as harsh winters, hot summers, droughts, and late summer cloudbursts.

The Pueblo peoples are the descendants of the Anasazi who, along with the Hohokam and the Mogollon, were one of the major cultural groups in the prehistoric Southwest. The history of the Anasazi and Pueblo peoples represents a continuous development of nearly 2000 years. Archaeologists have divided this development into periods based on specific cultural features. The cultural timeline begins with the Basketmaker I (BM I) period, which actually corresponds with the Archaic Period. In the BM II and BM III periods small farming communities developed. Made up of separated, single room living units dug into the ground and lined with stone slabs, these semi-subterranean structures, called pit houses, are probably the prototype for kivas. Kivas are usually round, semi-subterranean chambers used primarily for religious activities which were developed in later periods and are still in use today.

Beginning with the Pueblo I (P I) period, small above-ground masonry structures with multiple rooms were constructed. Gradually, such structures grew larger with the increasing population and resulting social complexity. By the P III period there were single pueblo units with several hundred rooms and as many as five stories serving as the centers of a complex network of associated communities. In the late P III period, after 1200, these major centers, such as Chaco Canyon and Mesa Verde, were abandoned possibly because of drought and over utilization of the available resources. During the period of migration and reintegration that followed P IV, many Anasazi moved eastward to the Rio Grande valley and established many of the pueblos that are still in existence today. Other Anasazi moved to the Hopi mesas in Arizona, and still others founded the pueblos of Acoma and Zuni.

The P V period began with the establishment of Spanish settlements in the Southwest during the sixteenth and seventeenth centuries. At that time the Pueblo peoples numbered perhaps as many as 100,000 living in approximately 135 villages. Contact with Europeans placed a great deal of stress on the existing social institutions and produced dramatic changes in the Pueblo way of life. Newly introduced diseases and forced labor decimated the population. Missionaries attempted to eradicate the existing religious institutions which were able to survive only by emphasizing private rather than public displays.

By 1880 New Mexico had become part of the United States and the railroad had arrived, resulting in even more rapid changes to Pueblo life. These changes were brought on by tourism, the commercialization of Pueblo art and culture, and United States government policies. In the twentieth century the challenge has been for the Pueblo peoples to achieve some sort of independence and success despite the dominance and demands of modern American culture. Today, while these and other challenges remain, it is fortunate that the population has stabilized, the religious belief system has survived, and other traditional institutions within culture have been able to adapt, thus providing a dynamic future for the Pueblo peoples.

A.

Gallup Black-on-white Jar
Anazazi PIII
Height: 11¾″

Museum Appropriation

x-1975.17

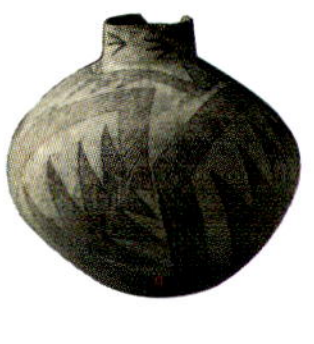

A.D. 200 300 400 500 600 700 800

(Archaic) Basketmaker II Basketmaker III Pueblo I

ARCHAEOLOGISTS BELIEVE that pottery first developed in the Southwest around A.D. 200, perhaps as a result of contact with the cultures to the south, in Mexico. The earliest pottery in the Southwest was utilitarian in nature, made primarily for cooking and food storage. The majority of these undecorated vessels were cooking pots, storage jars, and small pitchers, while there are a limited number of other forms such as scoops, canteens, and smoking pipes.

THE EXTERIORS OF THESE EARLY VESSELS were smoothed but not usually polished. Gradually, perhaps as decoration, there was a trend toward leaving evidence of the coils on utilitarian vessels instead of completely smoothing the surface. In addition to the decorative aspect, it is thought that not obliterating the coils on the exterior surface would enhance heat transfer during cooking, slow water evaporation, and provide a more secure grip for carrying. This intentional accentuation of the coils began with bands of coils around the neck during the late BM III and early P I periods, progressing to vessels with corrugated necks and to corrugation over the entire surface, until the P IV period, when the coils began to be completely obliterated again. The creation of unpainted utilitarian-type pottery continues today to a limited degree, primarily by some potters of the northern pueblos who make their vessels from micaceous clay, such as Lonnie Vigil (fig. B).

THE FIRST PAINTED POTTERY created by the Anasazi dates to around A.D. 550-575. The pottery of the BM III period featured designs consisting of narrow black lines painted in a loose, free-flowing style. The designs are often painted on the interior of small bowls and feature isolated figures with design layouts that are generally divided into quadrants. Throughout the P I and P II periods, the painted decoration became more structured and was organized with framed bands that were filled with geometric motifs arranged in symmetrical patterns. P III pottery is noted for a greater variety of forms such as canteens, mugs, pitchers, and even effigy forms. There is also greater emphasis on jars rather than bowls. While still adhering to a design layout developing in previous periods of dividing the design into quadrants, there was a tendency for a larger percentage of the surface on P III vessels to be painted. Each design was calculated to integrate with the vessel form, and the motifs were carefully executed with tight angular or curved black lines on the white slip ground. Until this period, the majority of painted decoration had been black on a white slip. However during this period the use of black painted designs on a red slip was developed. It is from this black-on-red style that white paint was added to the design and the first polychrome designs emerged.

BY THE P III PERIOD regional pottery styles with distinct characteristics had fully developed. In the Chaco Canyon region a high percentage of pottery forms from this period are jars (fig. A), including a unique type of flat-bottomed jar made in the form of a cylinder. The surfaces of Chacoan vessels are usually not very highly polished and are decorated with paint made from iron-bearing minerals. The mineral-based paint tends to produce a hard-edged line and sometimes exhibits a reddish tone after being fired, thus making it quite distinguishable. By comparison, the pottery forms made in the Mesa Verde region include mugs that are not common to any other region. The surfaces of Mesa Verde vessels tend to be highly polished and decorated with a carbon-based paint made from vegetal material. This paint tends to have a gray tone and produces a relatively softer edge.

THE P IV PERIOD WAS A TIME of dynamic change in the Southwest because the major regional centers, such as Chaco Canyon and Mesa Verde, were abandoned and new villages were established. This dynamic situation is reflected in the remarkable developments of P IV pottery. After A.D. 1300 an abundance of polychrome pottery was produced in a variety of distinctive shapes. Bowls tended to be larger and shallower with designs painted on both the interior and exterior. The predominant new jar shape was a low-slung vessel with a wide mouth and a broad shoulder that was the focus of the design. The designs painted on these vessels are frequently large, isolated images and often incorporate innovative figurative motifs: the avanyu (horned serpent) and masked figures that refer to ritual activities.

THE INNOVATIONS SEEN ON P IV POTTERY provided the foundations for pottery of the historic period. However, espe-

900 1000 1100 1200 1300 1400 1500 1600

PUEBLO II PUEBLO III PUEBLO IV HISTORIC ERA

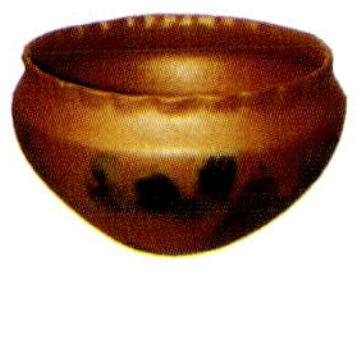

B.
MICACEOUS BOWL
LONNIE VIGIL
1991
Height: 7¾″

Gift of Lynn Bilotta and Stephen Bonadies in honor of Sara Wolf

1991.263

cially after the opening of the Santa Fe trail in the 1820s, one of the features of this historic period was the introduction of manufactured trade goods to the pueblos, resulting in a reduction in pottery production. Despite the reduction in pottery production, many of the ideal materials, vessel forms, and painted designs that constitute each Pueblo's traditional style of pottery were established by 1880.

After 1880, with the arrival of the railroad and even continuing on through today, there has been a revival of pottery production. This revival has been due to the fact that anthropologists and museum collectors purchased tens of thousands of vessels between 1880 and 1910. It has also been due in part to private collectors and tourists who purchase pottery as souvenirs of their visit to the Southwest. Such demands for pottery has created a new market which, in the last one hundred years, has shifted the paradigm so that most pottery is now made for external consumption rather than for use within the pueblo. Now there are countless gift shops and galleries established to sell to the casual tourist, while many private dealers cater to the serious collector.

In their quest to capitalize on the current marketability of pueblo pottery, many individuals have abandoned the difficult, time-consuming methods of making traditional pottery. In many instances, potters no longer dig their own clay, construct their vessels by hand, process their paint, and fire their pottery in the open (see *Pottery Techniques*). As a consequence, much of the pottery currently available on the market is made using non-traditional methods. Often individuals will purchase slip-cast pottery, called greenware, that was made in molds. The greenware is then painted, usually with ceramic or acrylic paints, available commercially, and fired in an electric kiln.

Fortunately the art of creating traditional pueblo pottery has not been lost. There are still potters at each pueblo who create pottery vessels in the same manner as their ancestors. They dig their own clay, form the vessel by hand, process their own paint from natural materials, and fire in the open. While some pueblos have more traditional potters than others, it is gratifying to realize that there is a young generation — like Virgil Ortiz (Cochiti), Rita Donna Martinez (San Ildefonso), Autumn Borts (Santa Clara), and Max Early (Laguna) — who create dynamic pottery expressions using traditional methods.

While the distinction between traditional and non-traditional pottery is primarily in the methods used to create the vessels, the real difference is embodied in the emphasis on the pottery-making process. By emphasizing the process, which has been handed down from generation to generation, traditional pottery-making serves as a vital link to the rich cultural heritage of the Pueblo people and also becomes a way of life for those who continue to create traditional pottery. This connection with the past is reflected in each traditionally made vessel which becomes not just the result of a single individual, but is the creation of countless generations of Pueblo potters. The traditional process of creating pottery, therefore, provides a way for individuals to remain in touch with their cultural traditions in a manner that ensures the continuation of Pueblo Indian art and culture well into the future.

Pottery Techniques

The most important aspect of traditional pueblo pottery is the process by which the vessels are created. It is a labor-intensive process, utilizing the same knowledge, techniques, and materials that have been developed and passed down from generation to generation. The raw clay must be dug out of the ground by hand and then processed. Stones, sand, and vegetal materials must be gathered and processed into paint. Old potsherds, sand, or volcanic ash must be gathered and processed into temper. Tools for molding the clay into the proper vessels shapes must be made and cared for. Fuel for firing the raw vessels must be gathered and dried. Because creating traditional pottery is so labor-intensive, the artists must be very devoted to the process. Therefore, making traditional pottery becomes a way of life that connects potters not only with their own creativity but also with their environment and cultural heritage.

The use of clay deposits throughout the Southwest is generally communal in nature, and each site is carefully monitored to ensure the proper use and respect for the precious material. Good deposits may be located a considerable distance from the pueblo and carrying the clay home can be a formidable undertaking, one that is accompanied by prayers. The different mineral content of each clay source produces its own unique results when it is fired. Hopi clay fires to a warm yellow-orange color while clay used by traditional potters at Zuni, Acoma, and Laguna fires to an off-white. Potters at Cochiti, Zia, Santo Domingo, Santa Clara, San Ildefonso, and Tesuque use a variety of clays that fire to gray, white, or red; and potters at Taos, Picuris, and the other northern pueblos have traditionally used mica-filled clay, which gives the vessels a sparkling quality.

ONCE THE CLAY IS ACCUMULATED it must be processed. It is ground to a powder in a stone mortar (metate) with a hand grinding-stone (mano). After the clay has been ground, it is soaked in water and the impure sediments are removed. The cleaned clay is then mixed with temper in order to give it elasticity and to prevent it from cracking when fired. There are a variety of materials that are used for temper. Crushed potsherds are used at Acoma and Laguna; sherds or sand or a combination of both at Zuni; sand at Hopi; and crushed basalt at Zia, Cochiti, and Santo Domingo. The potters who live at the pueblos on and near the Pajarito Plateau — such as Santa Clara and San Ildefonso — use ground volcanic tuff; at Tesuque, Taos, and Picuris the mica in the clay acts as a temper. Once the temper is mixed into the clay, the paste is rolled into balls and stored for future use.

THE VEGETAL AND MINERAL MATERIALS used for paint must also be gathered and processed. Generally red, orange, and yellow paint are obtained from naturally occurring iron-ore deposits such as hematite and limonite. Black, which fires to a variety of shades, from true black to a warm brown, can be obtained from iron-ore with beeweed often used as a binder. Beeweed is a wild plant harvested by potters for its leaves, which boil down to a thick tar-like consistency and, when mixed with rainwater, can be used as black or combined with other colors as a binder.

A VESSEL IS BEGUN by taking the paste and working it by hand into a pancake shape. The pancake is then placed into a mold called a puki, forming the base for the vessel. Rope-like coils of clay are added to build up the walls. The coils are pressed together and scraped on the inside and outside with an oval-shaped piece of gourd. The scraping process thins and smooths the walls, giving the vessel its final form. When the walls are pushed out and the rim evened, the vessel is then put aside to dry.

THE DRY VESSEL is coated with slip, a watery mixture of clay that acts as an undercoat for the painted decoration. It is usually applied with a rag in several coats. Once dry the slip is polished with a smooth, wet stone. Good polishing stones are highly prized and often handed down from generation to generation.

PAINTING TAKES PLACE after the vessel has been polished. The design is carefully laid out and lightly outlined in pencil — which burns off in the firing — over the entire surface. The paint is applied with brushes made of yucca leaves that have been chewed to expose their inner fibers. The outline of the design is painted, then the solid areas are filled in with color. Oftentimes children and younger potters are given the responsibility of painting in the solid areas for older family members, thus helping to perpetuate the knowledge of traditional pottery-making techniques. The vessel is put aside to dry after the painting is completed.

AFTER A VESSEL IS PAINTED and has been allowed to dry, it is ready to be fired, a process that hardens the clay and makes it durable. The firing process is tricky because moisture, air bubbles, or weak spots may cause the vessel to crack or explode. Even the best potters may lose up to ten percent of their vessels during the firing. In a traditional outdoor firing, an area is selected that is protected from the wind. A layer of sheep dung, used as fuel, is placed on the ground and a metal grate is set upon it. The pottery is carefully placed upon the grate and then covered with large potsherds to protect it from direct contact with the burning fuel. More sheep dung and/or small pieces of wood are placed over the potsherds until there is a beehive-shaped pile. If burning pieces of fuel come into limited contact with the vessels, the result is darkened areas on the surface referred to as fire clouds. Fire clouds are not seen as blemishes; instead they are often regarded as features that add character to a vessel.

IN THE OXYGENATED FIRING PROCESS, which is used at most pueblos, the fuel is lit and the fire allowed to burn itself out, a process which takes between forty-five minutes and an hour. In the oxygen-reduction firing process, often practiced at Santa Clara, San Ildefonso, and San Juan, the whole fire is smothered with additional dung after having burned for a time. This causes the entire surface of the vessel to turn black. After the fire has burnt out, the pottery is carefully removed and allowed to cool, thus completing the creation of traditional pueblo pottery.

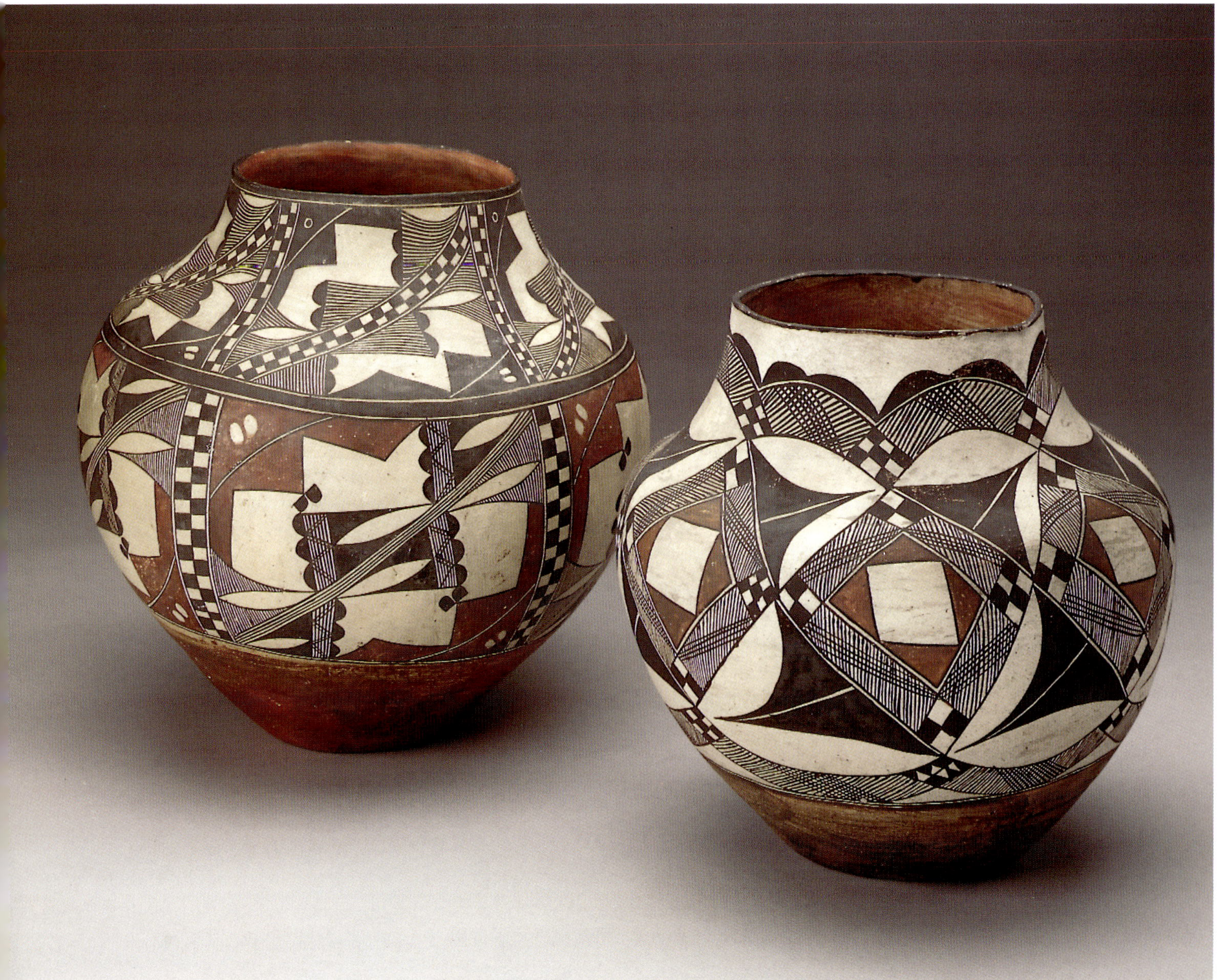

▲
1

Polychrome Jar
ca.1900
Height: 12¼″
Gift of Dorothy Powers

1965.472

▲
2

Polychrome Jar
ca.1900
Height: 10½″
Gift of Dorothy Powers

1965.471

Acoma

The Pueblo of Acoma is home to a very active community of potters. Traditionally, Acoma pottery is characterized by its thin, hard-fired walls and its light weight. High-shouldered jars are the most common form produced by Acoma potters, although bowls and canteens are also frequently made (figs. 7-9). The elegant forms are produced with smooth curves that show a graceful transition from one section of the body to another. The walls of Acoma vessels are generally much thinner that the pottery from any other Pueblo. The ability of Acoma potters to make vessels with such thin walls is due in large part to the clay. The white clay used by Acoma potters is very durable and, when mixed with ground sherds for temper and then fired, becomes a water-tight container that can withstand such modern uses as being placed in a microwave.

Acoma vessels are usually covered with a white slip and then painted. The designs are painted either in an all-over pattern (fig. 2) or into horizontal zones extending from the rim to the underbody (fig. 10). Traditional designs tend to be intricate, carefully painted patterns of repeated geometrical and curvilinear motifs executed in black, red/orange, and yellow. The designs may not be symmetrical but are usually fairly well balanced and complement the shaped of the vessel. Fine-line hatching is commonly used as a decorative element to fill outlined areas (fig. 1, 2). In addition to the complicated geometric designs, traditional Acoma designs may also include parrots, recognizable by their curved beaks (fig. 4), and flowering plants.

A twentieth-century innovation for Acoma potters, led by the Lewis and Chino families, is the use of the distinctive bold- and fine-line black-on-white designs from prehistoric Mimbres and Tularosa pottery on traditional Acoma vessels. Delores Lewis Garcia has noted that "our family would buy books to look up old pottery designs, and Dr. Kenneth Chapman from the Museum of New Mexico suggested to us to use the Mimbres designs and they

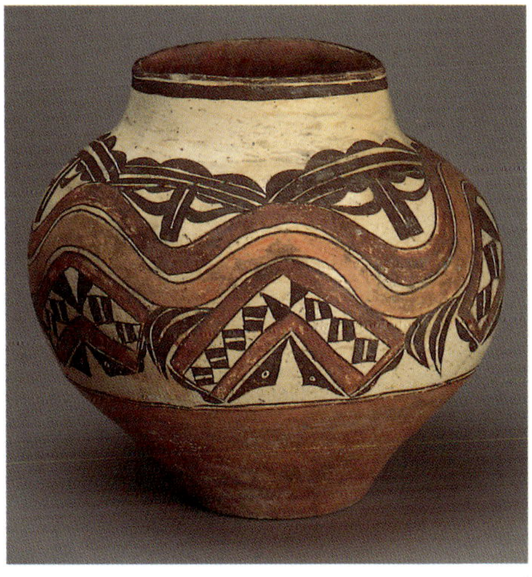

◀ 3

Polychrome Jar
ca.1880
Height: 11¾″

Collected by James Stevenson
Gift of the Women's Art Museum Association through exchange with the United States National Museum

1885.46

have become very popular for us today."(Maxwell Museum, 1991:9) According to Rose Chino Garcia in 1974, "the fine-line design we use a lot was revived by my aunt who found a sherd and gave it to my mother to use" (Maxwell Museum, 1991:3).

Although there is currently an active group of Acoma potters, not all of them work in the traditional manner. Those who create traditional pottery — like Maria "Lilly" Salvador, who has her own pottery gallery at the foot of the old pueblo — often use as their inspiration older Acoma pottery they have seen in museums, private collections, and exhibition catalogues (fig. 13). Frequently they

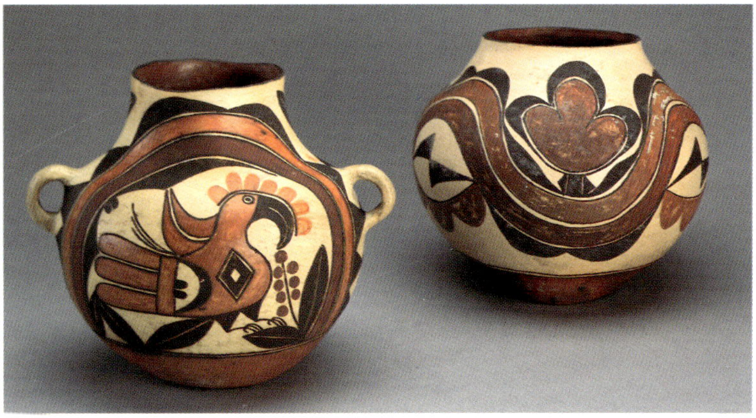

▲
4

Polychrome Jar
ca.1900
Height: 9″
Gift of
William N. King

1906.62

▲
5

Polychrome Jar
ca.1900
Height: 8¾″
Gift of
William N. King

1906.61

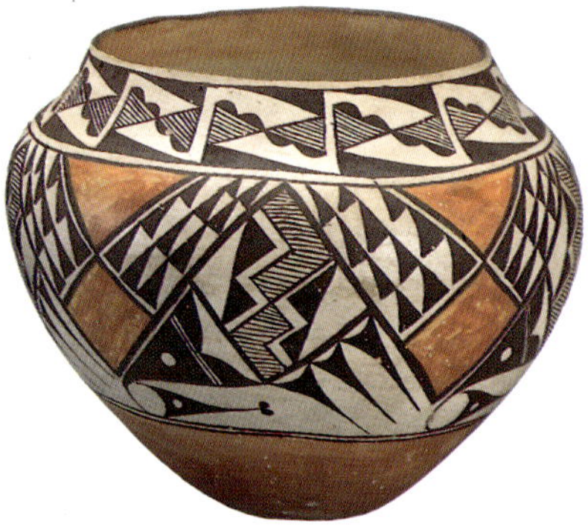

▲
6

Polychrome Jar
ca. 1960
Diameter: 7½″
Museum Purchase:
Gift of Mrs. Hugh Smythe
and Rebecca Scarborough,
by exchange

1994.25

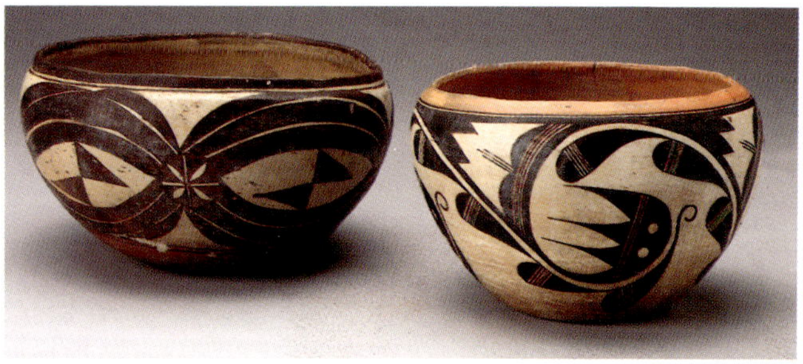

▶
7

Polychrome Bowl
ca. 1880
Diameter: 10″
Collected By James Stevenson
Gift of the Women's Art Museum
Association through exchange with
the United States National Museum

1885.58

▲
8

Polychrome Bowl
ca. 1950
Diameter: 8½″
Museum Purchase:
Gift of Herbert A. Faber,
by exchange

1994.28

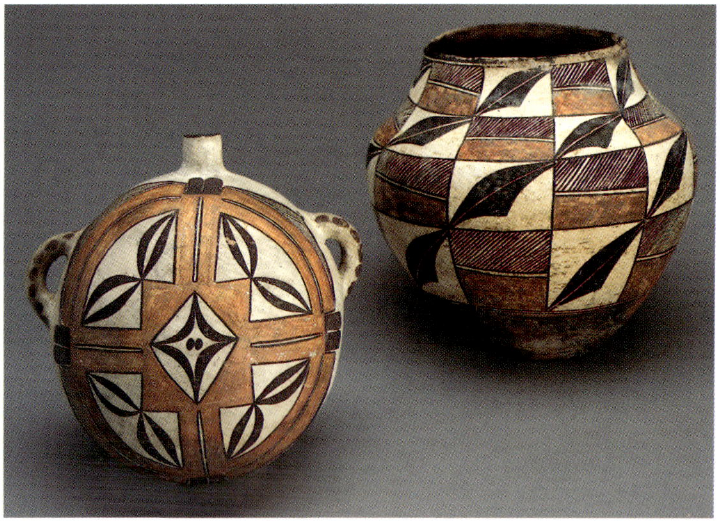

▶
9

Polychrome Canteen
ca.1880
Height: 9¾″
Collected by James Stevenson
Gift of the Women's Art
Museum Association through
exchange with the United
States National Museum

1885.64

◀
10

Polychrome Jar
ca.1900
Height: 11″
Gift of
Amelia Elizabeth White

1937.525

will reuse designs from historic vessels, thus emphasizing the connection between historic and contemporary traditonal Accoma pottery. Like Maria Salvador, Mary Lewis Garcia also comes from a well-known family of Acoma potters. Her mother was the famous potter Lucy Lewis, and several of her sisters are also active in pottery-making. Mary prefers to use traditional Acoma designs on her elegantly shaped vessels (figs. 11, 14): "I like the old Acoma designs the best. There's just some-thing special about them. That's why I like to use them on my pottery."

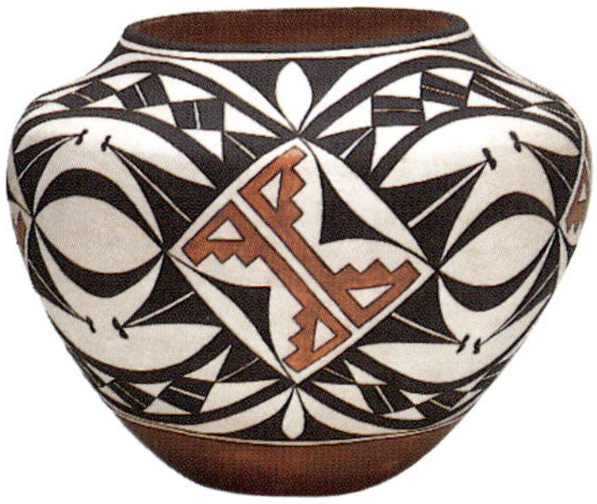

▲
11

POLYCHROME JAR
Mary Lewis Garcia
1994
Height: 9½″

Museum Purchase: Gift of Mr. and Mrs. L. Harold Wehling; Daniel and Irene Randolph; Charles and Harriet Edwards

1994.243

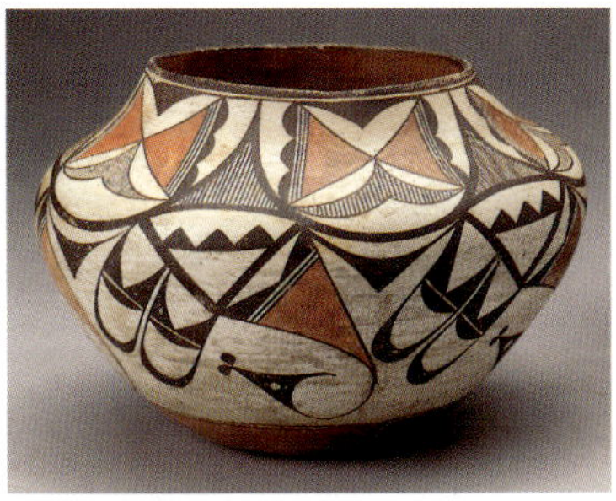

▲
12

POLYCHROME JAR
ca. 1950
Height: 7½″

Museum Purchase: Gift of Herbert A. Faber, by exchange

1994.26

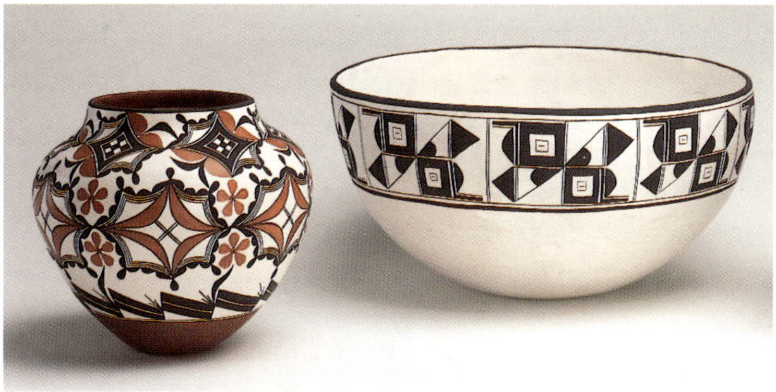

▲
13

POLYCHROME JAR
Maria "Lilly" Salvador
1994
Height: 8″

Museum Purchase: Gift of Dabby Blatt

1994.245

▲
14

BLACK-ON-WHITE BOWL
Mary Lewis Garcia
1994
Diameter: 15″

Museum Purchase: Gift of James Edgy and Robert Lee; Angela Campbell

1994.244

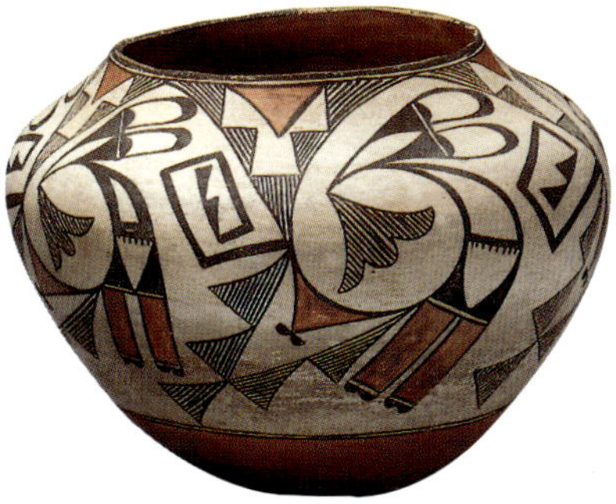

▲
15

POLYCHROME JAR
ca. 1950
Height: 8½″

Museum Purchase: Gift of Herbert A. Faber, by exchange

1994.27

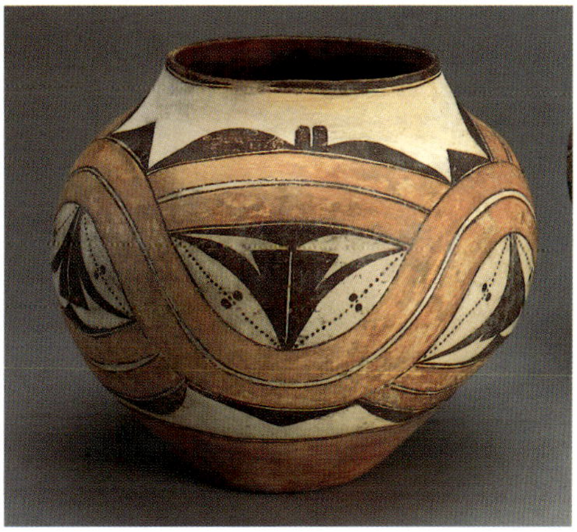

◄
16

POLYCHROME JAR
ca.1880
Height: 11¾″

Collected by James Stevenson Gift of the Women's Art Museum Association through exchange with the United States National Museum

1885.47

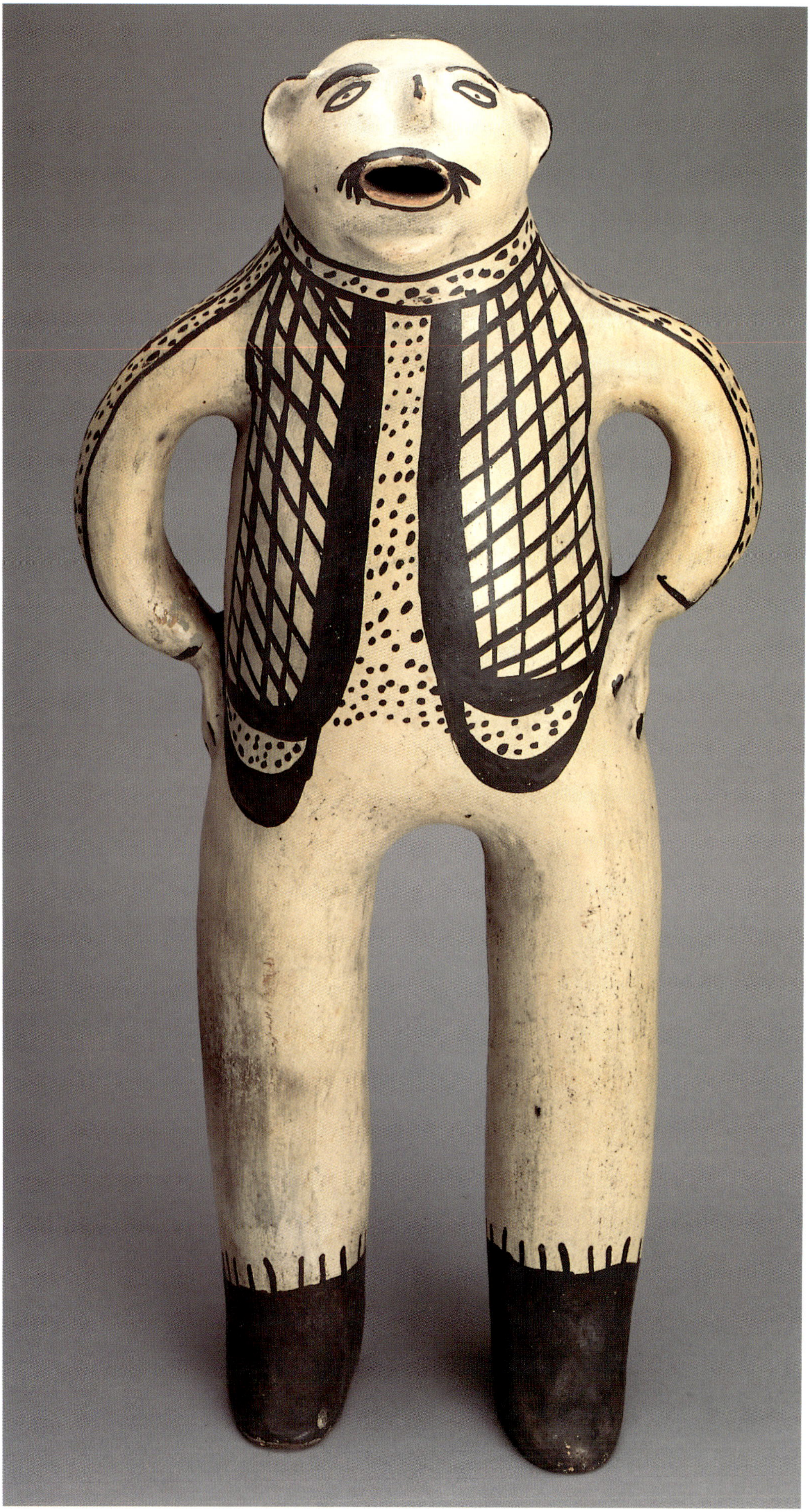

▶
17

Polychrome Figure
ca.1900
Height: 21″

Gift of
Mary Hanna

1915.45

Cochiti

Traditionally, the pottery created at Cochiti Pueblo is produced in a wide range of forms, including vessels made in the shape of birds and human figures. Cochiti jars tend to be spherical in shape and may have a flared rim. Bowls are similar in shape to those produced at nearby Santo Domingo but are not nearly as large. Pitchers are another common form. Decoration usually consists of black-painted designs on a white or gray slip with a red-slipped underbody. The same red slip is applied to the interior of bowls. Sometimes red paint is also used in the design as a highlight or filler. The painted design is located on vessels within an area framed by black lines. A characteristic line break is usually placed in the framing line around the rim. Although the design field is framed at the top and the bottom, it is not usually divided into panels; thus, the images are isolated and seem to float on the surface of the vessel.

The designs on Cochiti pottery are generally executed in loose, fluid brushstrokes that are fairly thick and may appear to be rather quickly applied. Floral motifs are frequently depicted, often in association with birds and geometric forms. Also common are representations of clouds, lightning, rain, and the avanyu, or water serpent, which are all considered to be important symbols.

Perhaps the best-known Cochiti forms are human figures. Figurative pottery has been made at Cochiti since before the turn of the century. Birds (fig. 18) and other animals are common forms, but human figures are the most distinctive. Earlier in the this century it was common for Cochiti potters to create large, free-standing figures that represented Hispanics or Anglos (fig. 17). These figures were often satirical representations and many of them depicted such larger-than-life individuals as opera singers and circus performers. Creating such representations, although originally encouraged by Santa Fe traders, was eventually discontinued by the 1920s. In the 1960s one Cochiti potter, Helen Cordero, began to create another type of figure which she referred to as a storyteller.

The most familiar type of storyteller is a seated man or woman posed as if telling a story, with

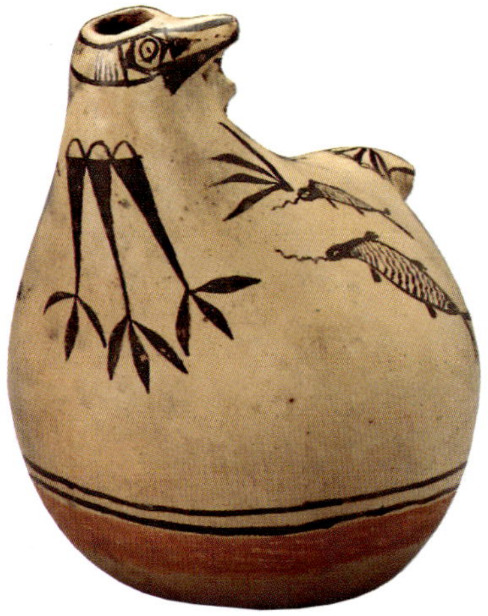

▲
18

Polychrome Bird Effigy Vessel
ca.1900
Height: 8″

Museum Appropriation
x-1976.1

as many as a dozen small children arranged on and around the storyteller. These figures have become extremely popular and are now made in some form by many Cochiti potters, most notably Louis and Virginia Naranjo, who continue to use traditional Cochiti clay, slip, and paint (fig. 22). Currently there are very few potters at Cochiti who produce traditional style bowls and jars. However Virgil Ortiz, who began making pottery when he was a child, is noted for creating jars decorated with the same bird designs painted on his mother's and grandmother's vessels (fig. 21). His is also well known for having revived the practice of creating such freestanding figures as opera singers and circus performers as well as his own more contemporary oriented figures (fig. 20).

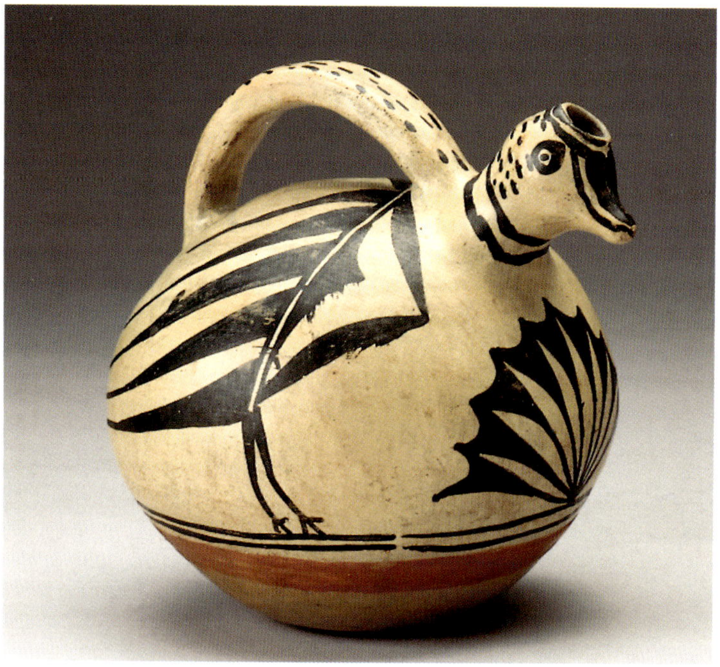

▲
19

POLYCHROME BIRD EFFIGY VESSEL
ca.1900
Height: 8″

Gift of William N. King

1906.65

20

Standing Figure
Virgil Ortiz
1994
Height: 12¾″

Museum Purchase:
Gift of
Norman A. Murdock:
Mr. and Mrs. Daniel Stricker

1994.246

21

Polychrome Jar
Virgil Ortiz
1994
Height: 8¾″

Museum Purchase:
Gift of
Mr. and Mrs. J. Richard Andre

1994.247

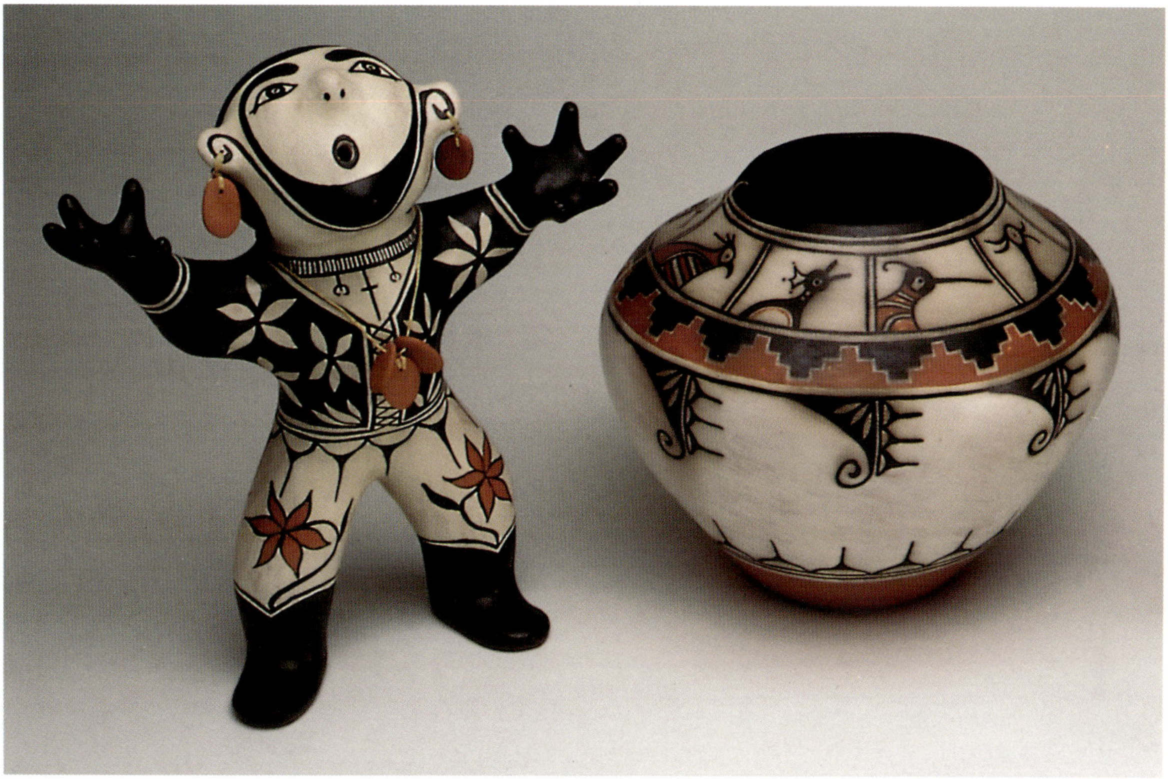

22

Storyteller Figure
Louis & Virginia Naranjo
1994
Height: 8¾″

Museum Purchase:
Gift of Julia R. Schiff

1994.248

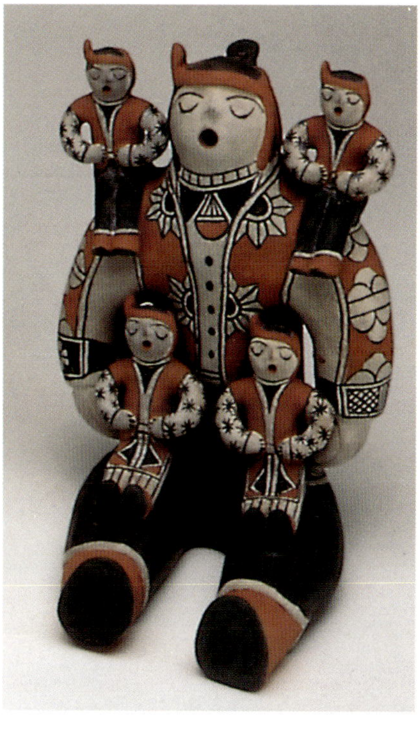

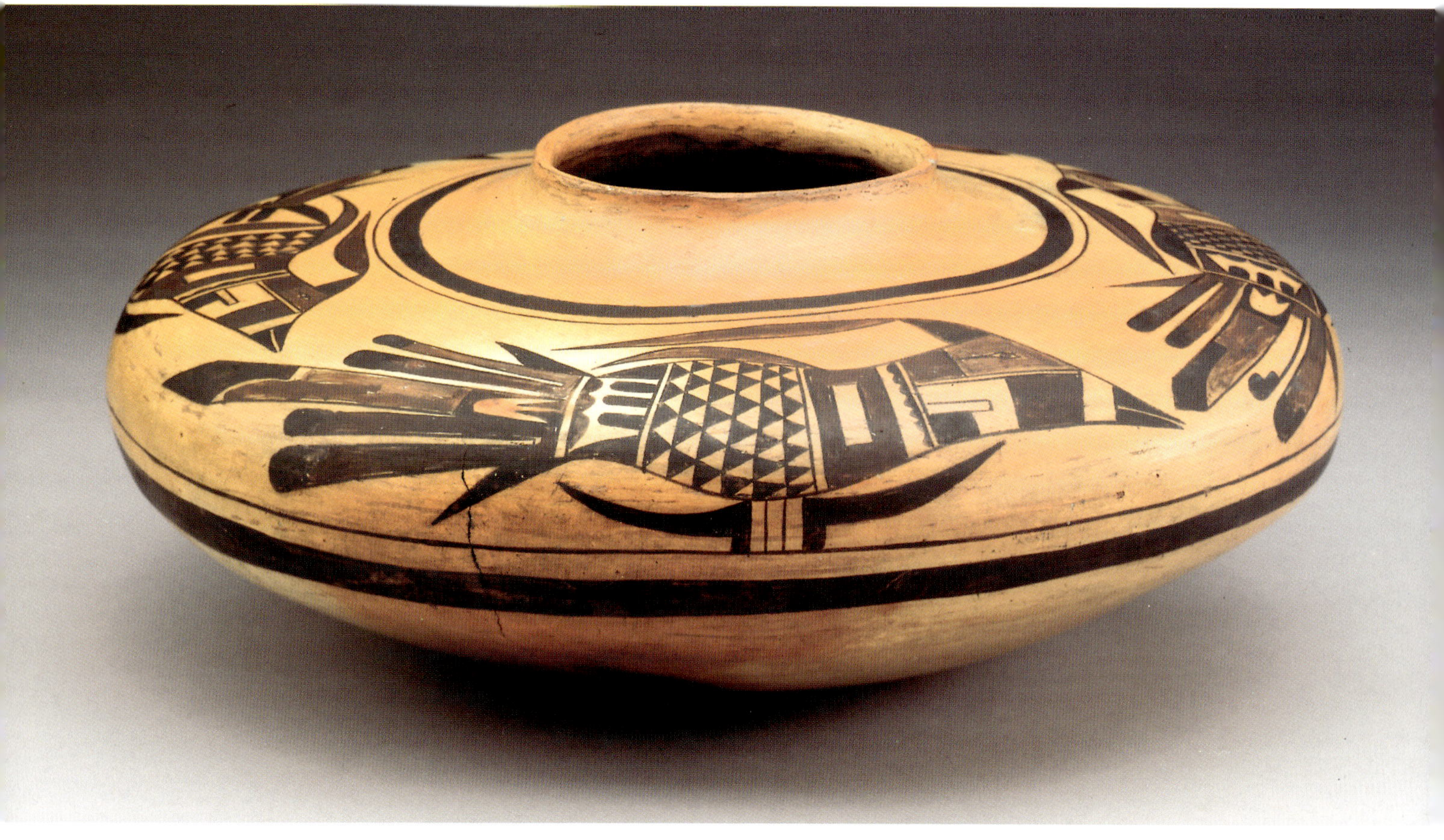

▲
23

POLYCHROME JAR
NAMPEYO (?)
ca.1900
Height: 7″

Museum Appropriation
x-1975.18

Hopi

Modern Hopi pottery is part of an extremely rich tradition that extends back to the prehistoric era. Characteristic vessel forms include shallow cowls, cylindrical shaped jars and flat low-slung jars having little or no neck. Hopi pottery is further distinguished by the unique polychrome designs painted on the vessels. Most Hopi pottery is unslipped and made with clay that, when fired, ranges from yellow to a deep, warm orange. Hopi potters fire their vessels at a comparatively high temperature which, when combined with the iron content in the clay and, when put in contact with bits of the burning fuel, can result in tonal variations on the surface. This variation in color is thought to add to the overall aesthetic quality of the vessel. Hopi pottery of the 1800s was basically utilitarian, made for use in the household. One of the most common types of Hopi pottery from this period is Polacca Polychrome. Typical forms include wide-mouthed globular-shaped jars and bowls with sharply flaring rims (fig. 25). These forms are visually similar to Zuni pottery produced at about the same time. The painted designs on Hopi pottery of the late 1800s is also similar to the abstract curvilinear and geometric designs on pottery from Zuni and the Rio Grande pueblos rather than the bird and feather motifs that were frequently painted on Hopi pottery of the late prehistoric and early historic periods.

Much of the Hopi pottery created in the last one hundred years can be traced back to the Sikyatki revival begun by the potter Nampeyo (fig 23). Sikyatki pottery was originally produced between 1375 and 1625 in the Hopi village of the same name. It is considered to be among the most elegant and appealing of prehistoric pottery of the Southwest. Between 1885 and 1890, at the urging of Jesse Walter Fewkes, an archaeologist, Nampeyo and others

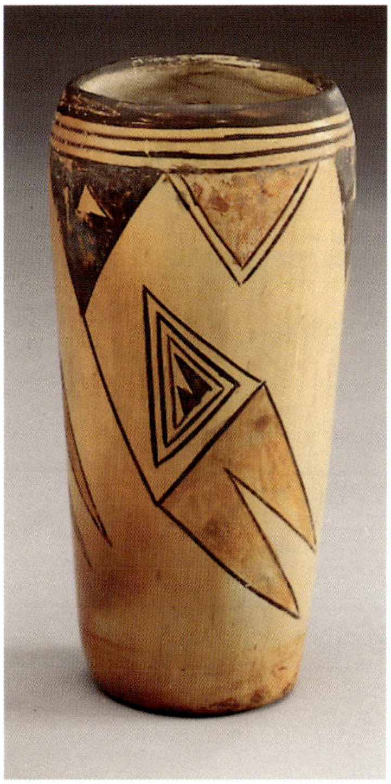

▲
24

Polychrome Cylinder Jar
ca.1930
Height: 6¼″

Gift of Dr. Daniel Cook

1943.925

began producing pottery in the same distinctive forms and painted with the same type of abstracted bird (fig 23), feather, and cloud motifs as the earlier Sikyatki vessels.

By reviving the older style of pottery, Nampeyo received a great deal of attention that in turn resulted in a florescence of Hopi pottery-making that still continues. Today, most Hopi pottery is created in the Sikyatki revival style. However, as Dextra Quotskuyva Nampeyo, a great-granddaughter of Nampeyo says, "I keep experimenting. I use a lot of my own designs, though I don't want to get away from the traditional" (SWAIA, 1991:34). Mark Tahbo is another noted potter who continues to create the forms that are unique to Hopi pottery (fig. 29). He is espe-

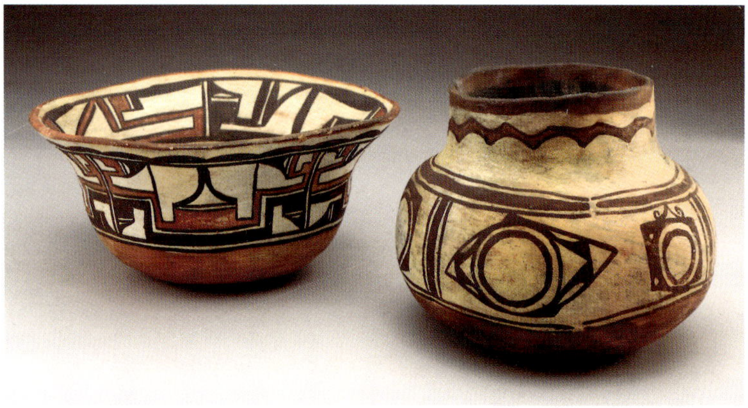

▲ 25

Polacca Polychrome Bowl
ca.1880
Diameter: 10½″

Collected by John Wesley Powell
Gift of the Women's Art Museum Association through exchange with the United States National Museum

1885.72

▲ 26

Polacca Polychrome Jar
ca.1880
Height: 7″

Gift of the Women's Art Museum Association through exchange with the United States National Museum

1885.55

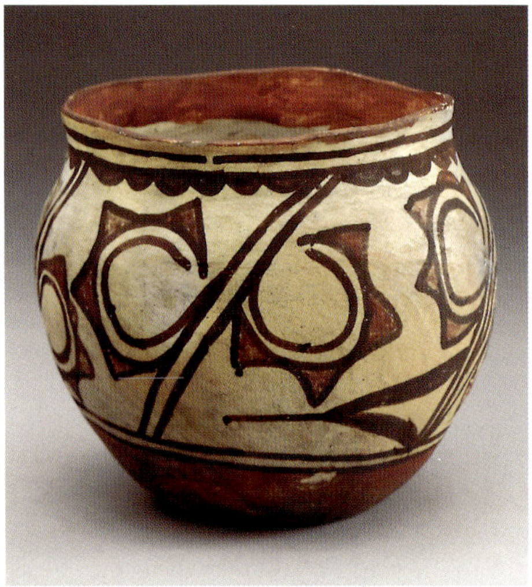

▲ 27

Polacca Polychrome Jar
ca. 1880
Height: 7¼″

Collected by Cosmos/Victor Mindeleff
Gift of the Women's Art Museum Association through exchange with the United Stated National Museum

1885.89

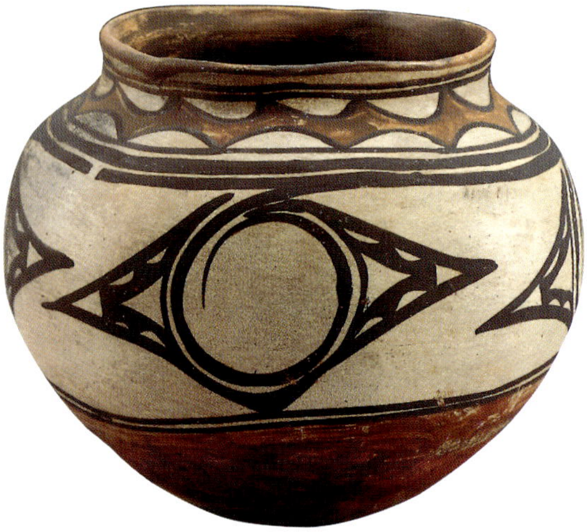

▲ 28

Polacca Polychrome Jar
ca. 1880
Height: 8¼″

Gift of the Women's Art Museum Association through exchange with the United Stated National Museum

1885.51

cially well known for the tonal range that he is able to achieve during the firing process. He sometimes emphasizes this color gradation by not painting designs on a vessel, thereby allowing the expressive fire clouds and range of colors produced by the firing to act as the decoration (fig. 30). Fawn Navasie Garcia, who comes from a well-known family of potters, also creates vessels with unique shapes and stylish designs that reflect the rich tradition of Hopi pottery (fig. 31).

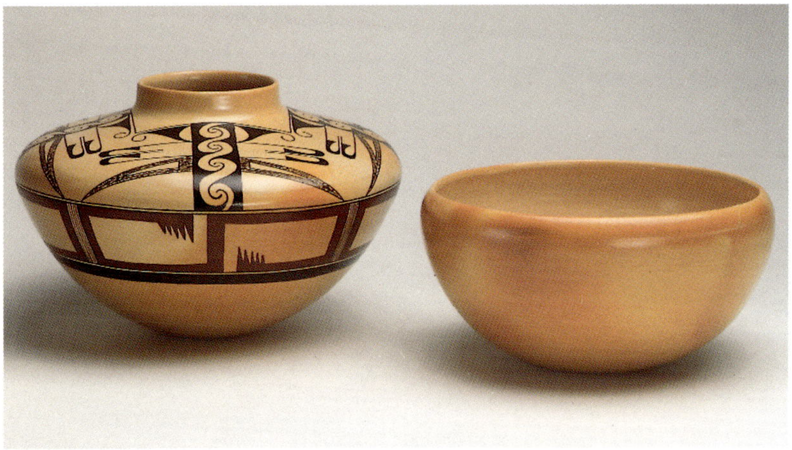

▲
29

POLYCHROME JAR
MARK TAHBO
1994
Height: 7½″

Museum Purchase:
Gift of Carol and
Theodore Striker

1994.250

▲
30

YELLOWWARE BOWL
MARK TAHBO
1994
Diameter: 10¼″

Museum Purchase:
Gift of Thomas R. Schiff;
Mr. and Mrs. Joseph H. Rohling

1994.249

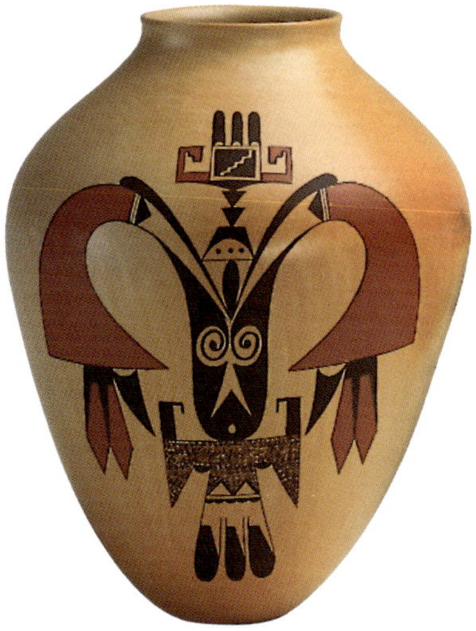

▲
31

POLYCHROME JAR
FAWN GARCIA
1994
Height: 11¼″

Museum Purchase:
Gift of Dabby Blatt

1994.251

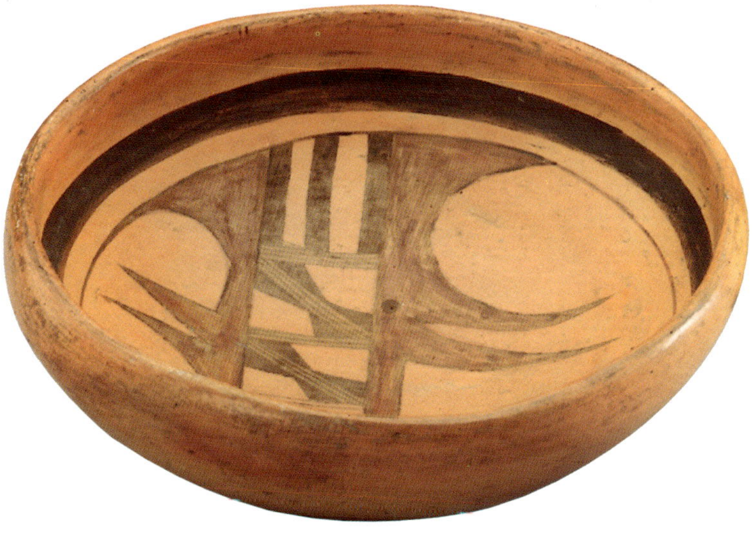

▲
32

POLYCHROME BOWL
ca. 1920
Diameter 7¾″

Museum Appropriation

x-1994.3

Laguna

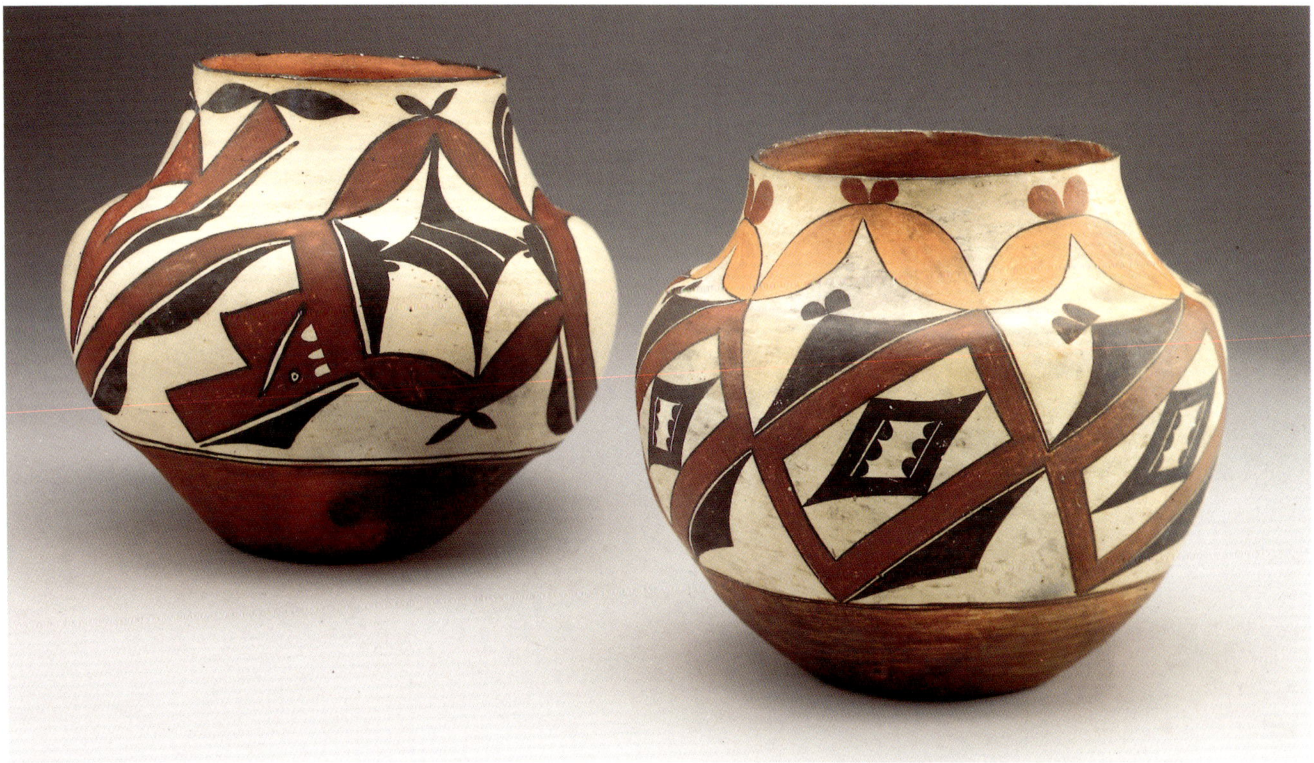

▲
33

Polychrome Jar
ca.1850
Height: 9¼″

Gift of William N. King

1906.59

▲
34
Polychrome Jar
ca.1890
Height: 8¾″

Gift of William N. King

1906.60

Laguna Pueblo, founded in the 1690s, is located approximately fourteen miles northeast of Acoma. Laguna was originally settled by people from various pueblos who moved first to Acoma following the Pueblo Revolt and the Spanish reoccupation of New Mexico. Laguna grew quickly and, less than a century later, was nearly as large as Acoma. Because of their proximity and their use of a common language, the people of Acoma and Laguna share many characteristics both culturally and historically.

Laguna pottery also frequently resembles the pottery of Acoma, especially jars which are often

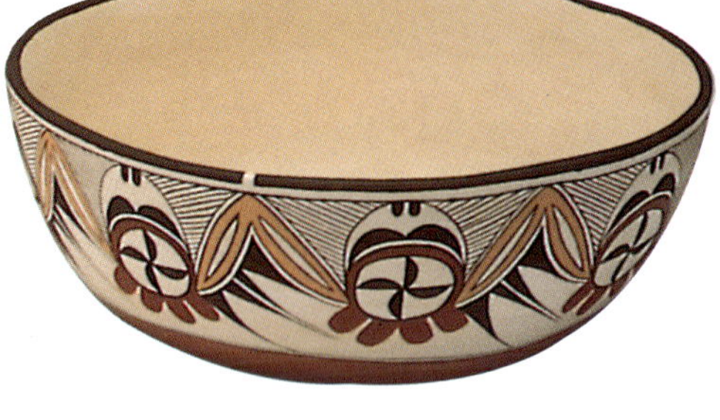

◀
35

Polychrome Bowl
Max Early
1994
Diameter: 11″

Museum Purchase:
Gift of Cathy T. Mitchell

1994.252

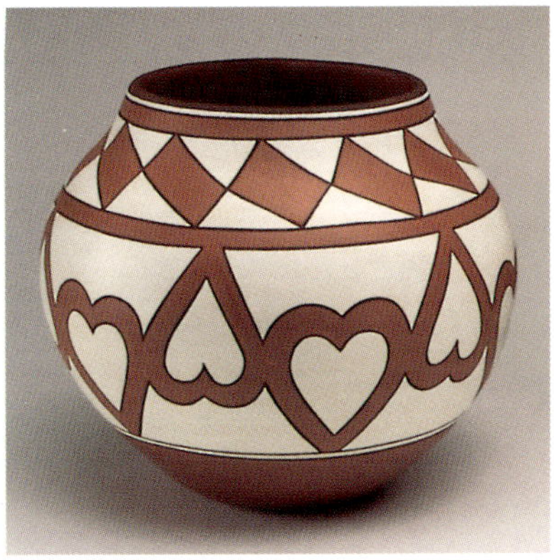

◀
36

Polychrome Jar
Gladys Paquin
1994
Height: 10⅝″
....
Museum Purchase:
Gift of
Gail and Fred Berger;
The Misses Hillary and
Megan Thompson

1994.127

similar both in terms of form and painted designs. As with Acoma pottery, the use of a white slip is favored, and the jars are generally constructed with the same high-shouldered shape. Care is also taken to ensure thin, sturdy walls. Typically, the polychrome designs on Laguna pottery reflect the intricate combinations of curvilinear, geometric, and floral designs similar to those found on traditional Acoma pottery.

In spite of the many similarities between traditional Acoma and Laguna pottery, there are several features that may be considered unique to Laguna pottery. The clay used at Laguna is judged to be slightly denser than the Acoma clay. While Acoma clay is mixed with crushed pot sherds for temper, Laguna potters, historically, are more likely to mix sand with the crushed pot sherds. The use of comparatively large interlocking motifs such as hearts or diamonds painted around the middle of the vessel is another feature that is often characteristic of Laguna pottery. At the points of connection, the orange or red is continuous and is not interrupted by the black outline (fig. 34).

The use of the interlocking heart design (fig. 36) continues to be used and admired by well-known Laguna potter Gladys Paquin, who has stated: "I think it's just their inspiration I wonder what this person thought about then they drew these things. I wonder what inspired this person to put these hearts on the pot" (Trimble, 1987:82). Like many other traditional potters Gladys Paquin often uses as reference older Laguna vessels in museum collection and books as her inspiration and has influenced other potters, like Max Early, to do the same. Max Early is a talented young potter who has been creating traditional Laguna style pottery with polychrome designs for only several years (fig. 35).

▶
37

Polychrome Jar
Gladys Paquin
1994
Height: 11½″
....
Museum Purchase:
Gift of
Dr. and Mrs. Sanford R. Courter

1994.128

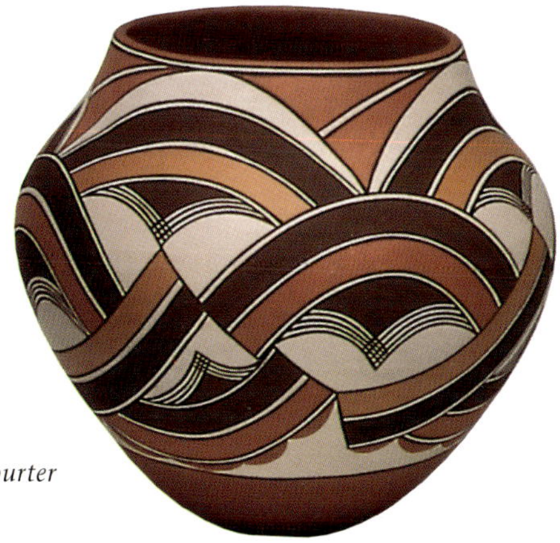

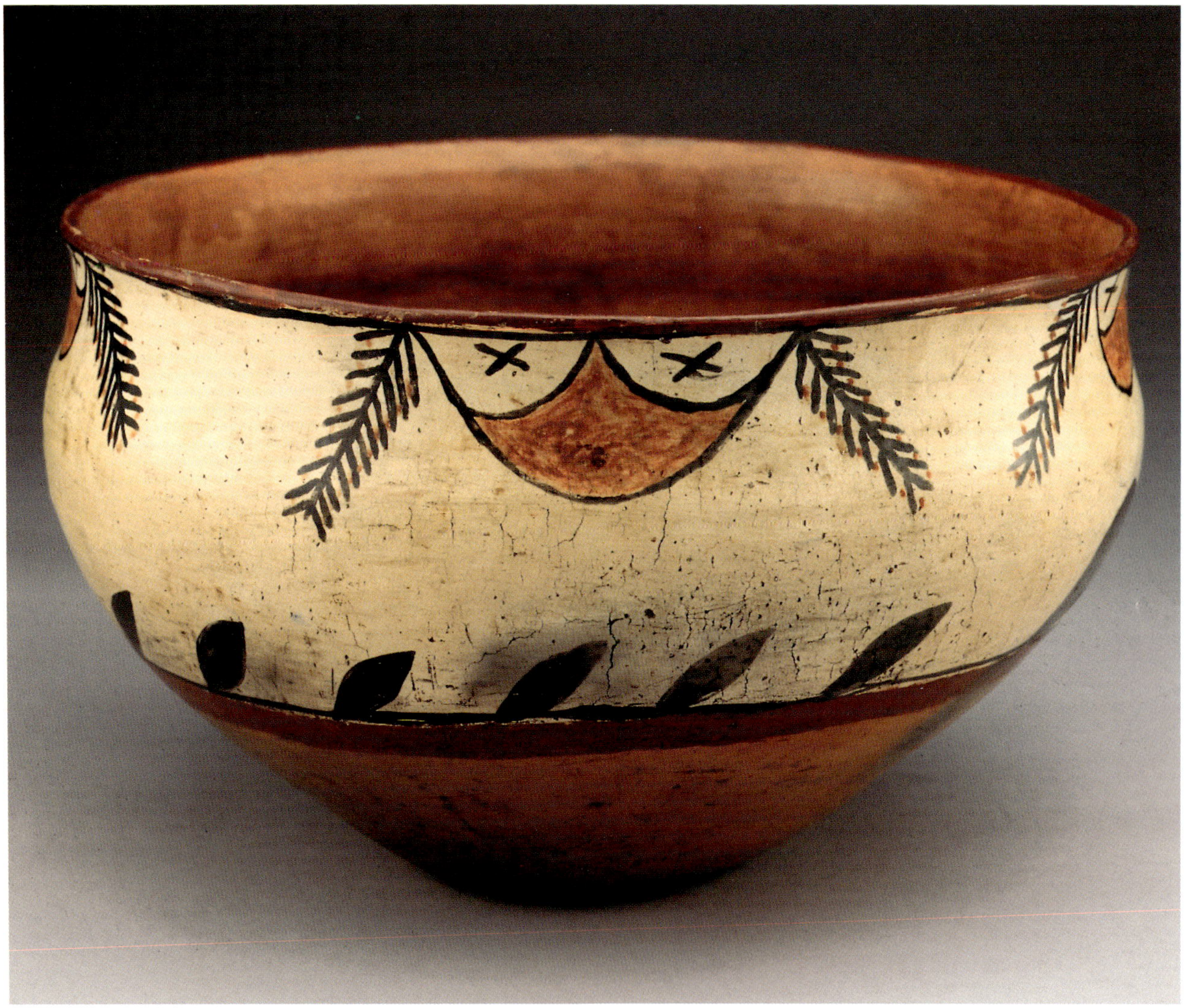

▲
38

Polychrome Bowl
ca.1900
Diameter: 15″

Museum Purchase:
Gift of
Dr. and Mrs.
Sanford R. Courter

1992.30

San Ildefonso

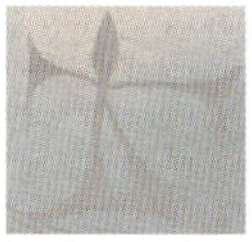

The pottery produced at San Ildefonso Pueblo first become famous early in the twentieth century as the source of black-on-black pottery, a style that developed around 1919 by Maria Martinez and her husband, Julian Martinez. Though polished black pottery was produced prior to that at nearby Santa Clara and San Juan pueblos, the Martinezes developed the technique of black matte paint on a polished black vessel made from the locally gathered red clay. The process consists of using black paint on the highly polished surface of the vessel and then firing it in an oxygen-reducing atmosphere. The result is a matte black painted design on a highly polished black surface. This black-on-black style immediately became popular with the buying public and is a technique that continues to be used by many San Ildefonso potters.

Following the lead of Maria and Julian Martinez and their family, San Ildefonso potters have developed a variety of forms and techniques now considered traditional. Some examples are unpainted, highly polished black or red vessels while others are matte cream painted designs on a polished red surface. Some of the most common forms are small jars (fig. 39), on which the painted designs are placed between the shoulder and the rim, and bowls, on which the painted decoration is located in a framed area on the exterior just below the rim. Plates are another form that are frequently created (figs. 43). The highly polished, slightly concave plates provide the ground for large painted motifs that cover the entire surface. Often the motifs painted on the plates, like those painted on other forms, are the avanyu (water serpent) or feather designs interpreted from the feather design painted on prehistoric Mimbres pottery.

Somewhat eclipsed by the popularity of black-on-black pottery, traditional pottery at San Ildefonso

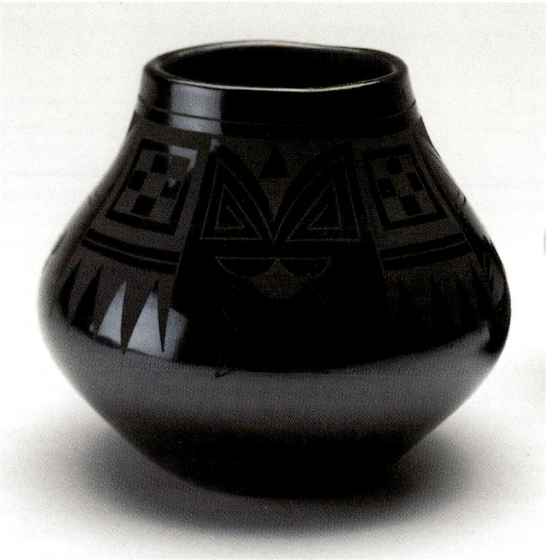

◀ 39

Black-on-black Jar
Margaret Lou Gutierrez and Elvis Torres
1994
Height: 6¼″

Museum Purchase: Gift of Robert and Lois Johannigman

1994.256

also includes a polychrome style with the designs painted on a tan-colored slip (fig. 38). This style features the use of red paint in the design, red paint around the rim, and an exceptionally smooth, stone-polished surface. A black-on-red style (fig. 46), no longer produced, was another traditional type of San Ildefonso pottery. Spherical shaped jars, sometimes constructed with inverted lips and lids, are the most common black-on-red forms. Pottery-making continues to be a dynamic artistic tradition at San Ildefonso. As Juan Tafoya (fig. 44) states, "I am very interested in continuing the art of pottery-making, which has been a part of my culture for hundreds of years and continues to be an expression of artistic creation as well as a

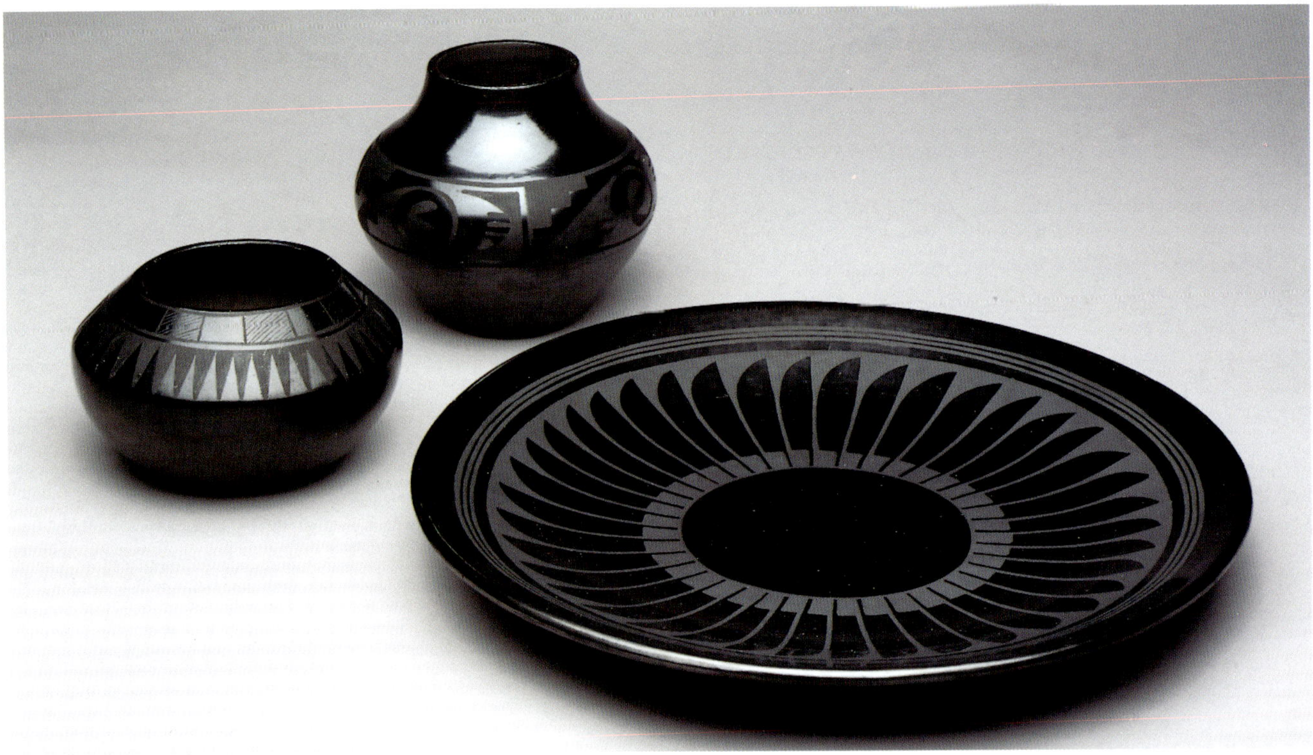

▲
40 *(left)*

Black-on-black Jar
Maria Martinez
ca. 1940
Height: 3½″

Gift of Dr. Daniel Cook

1943.924

▲
41 *(center)*

Black-on-black Jar
Santana Martinez
ca. 1930
Height: 5¼″

Gift of
Amelia Elizabeth White

1937.518

▶
42

Cream-on-red Jar
Albert & Josephine Vigil
1994
Height: 8¼″

Museum Purchase:
Gift of Sarah C. Schiff

1994.253

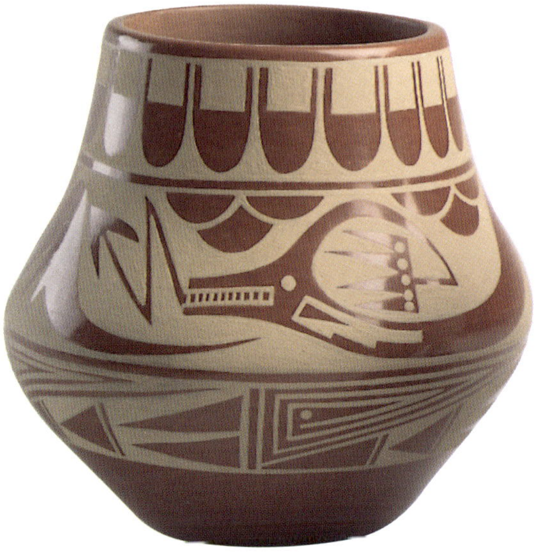

way of life for use today." Other noted San Ildefonso potters include Albert and Josephine Vigil, who learned to make San Ildefonso pottery from his aunt, Maria Martinez. The Vigils specialize in the cream-on-red style, with Josephine making the vessels and Albert painting them (fig. 42). Elvis Torres, nephew of famed potter Helen Gutierrez, is an historian of San Ildefonso pottery who began his artistic career as a painter. Now he creates small vessels on his own and occasionally paints designs on the pottery his aunt Margaret Lou Gutierrez creates (fig. 39). Another of Elvis' relatives, Kathy Gutierrez also makes pottery and frequently creates the unique double-shoulder jars that are also a part of the San Ildefonso pottery tradition (fig. 45).

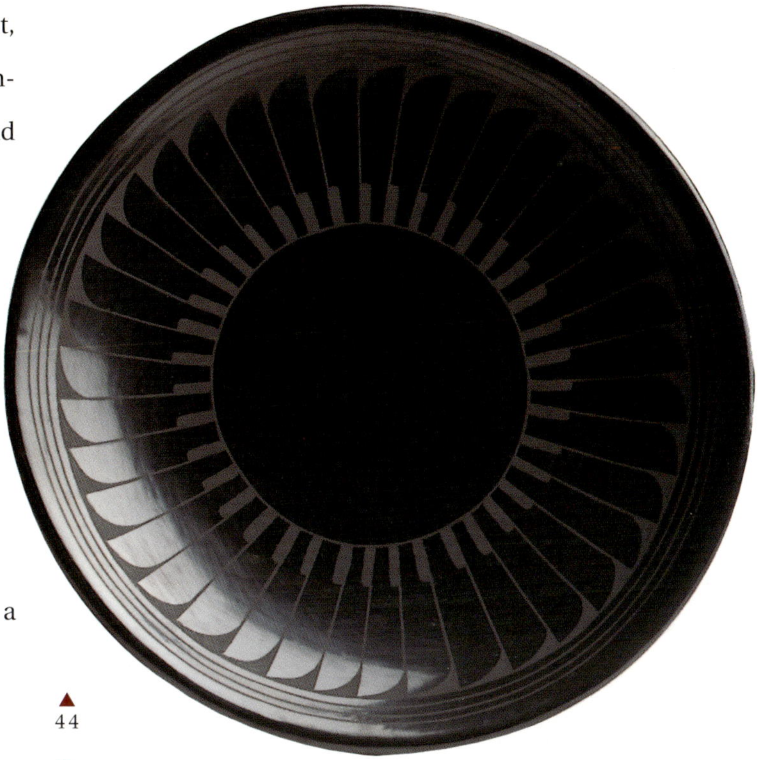

▲
44

BLACK-ON-BLACK PLATE
JUAN TAFOYA
1994
Diameter: 11½"

Museum Purchase:
Gift of Mr. and Mrs. L. Harold Wehling

1994.255

◄
43 *(right)*

BLACK-ON-BLACK PLATE
MARIA AND SANTANA MARTINEZ
ca. 1945
Diameter: 14¾"

Gift of Mrs. Howard Wurlitzer

1948.174

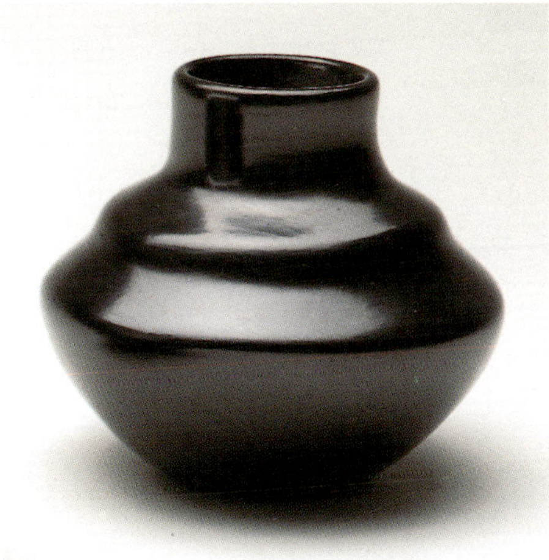

◄
45

POLISHED BLACK JAR
KATHY GUTIERREZ
1994
Height: 5¾"

Museum Purchase:
Gift of Stephanie Eha

1994.254

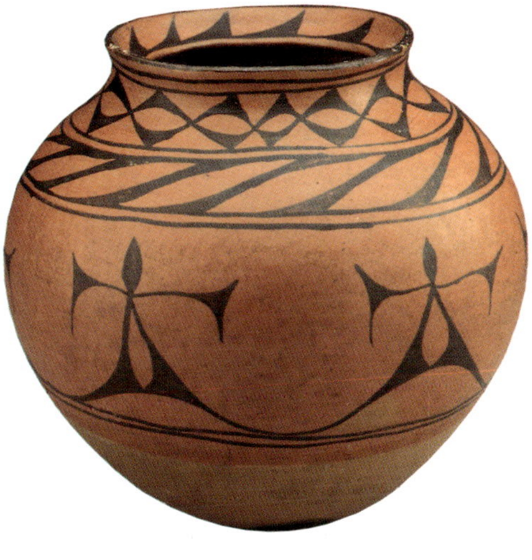

▲
46

BLACK-ON-RED JAR
ca.1880
Height: 10¼"

Museum Appropriation

x-1994.1

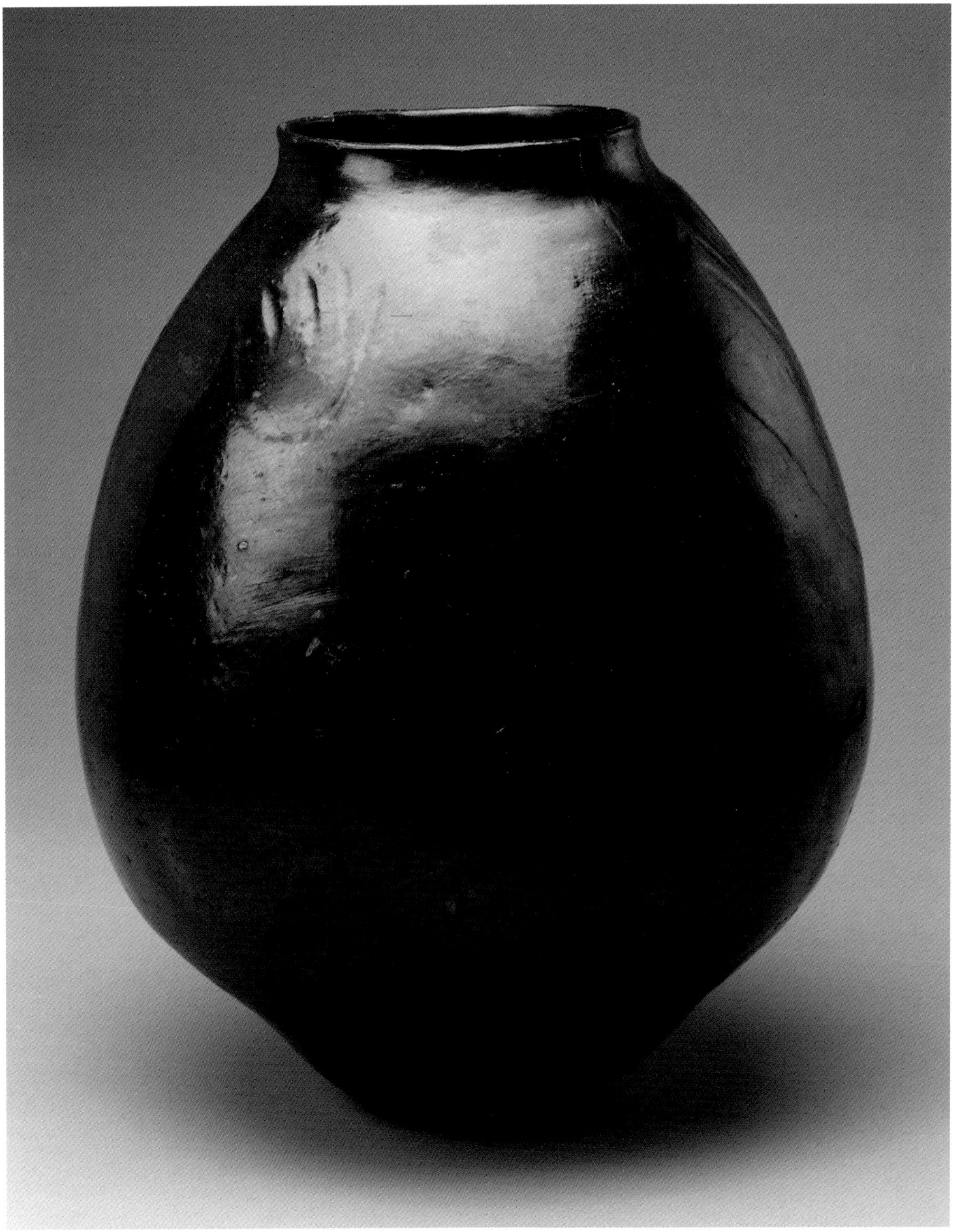

▲
47

POLISHED BLACKWARE JAR
ca. 1930
Height: 20½″

Gift of Amelia Elizabeth White

1937.527

Santa Clara

The dynamic pottery tradition of Santa Clara Pueblo features more potters who are responsible for more innovations than potters from any other pueblo. Historically, Santa Clara potters have been masters of form. Most traditional Santa Clara pottery is highly polished, unpainted black or red vessels with relatively thick walls. Often there is an emphasis placed on the creation of large, elegant vessels (fig. 47). Typical forms include bowls, long-necked jars, and large water storage jars with rounded bottoms (fig. 48). Another distinctive shape is the double-spouted wedding jar with a strap handle (fig. 49). These unique vessels appear to have first become common shortly after the turn of the century and remain popular gifts for newlyweds.

The decoration of Santa Clara pottery is as innovative as the distinctive forms. One decorative technique is to impress a design into the surface of the vessel before the clay has completely dried. Often the impressed design is in the shape of a bear paw, a reference to the belief that once, during a drought, a bear led the people of Santa Clara to water. In the 1920s carving designs into the thick walls of a vessel first became popular and, in some examples, the deeply carved designs

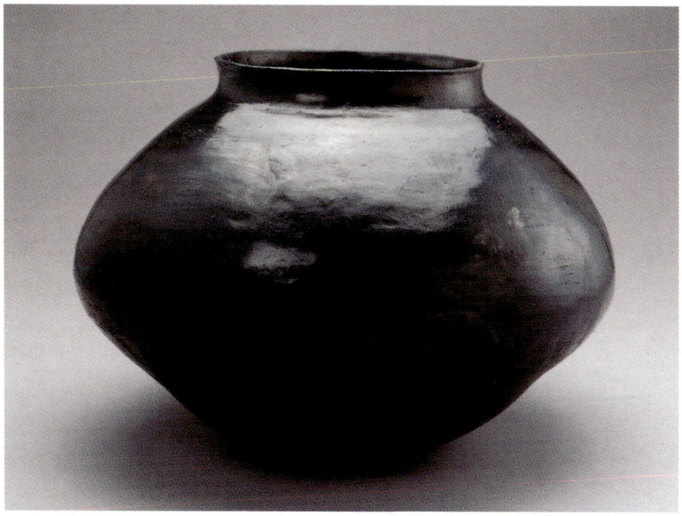

▲
48

Polished Blackware Jar
ca. 1930
Height: 16″

Gift of
Amelia Elizabeth White

1937.529

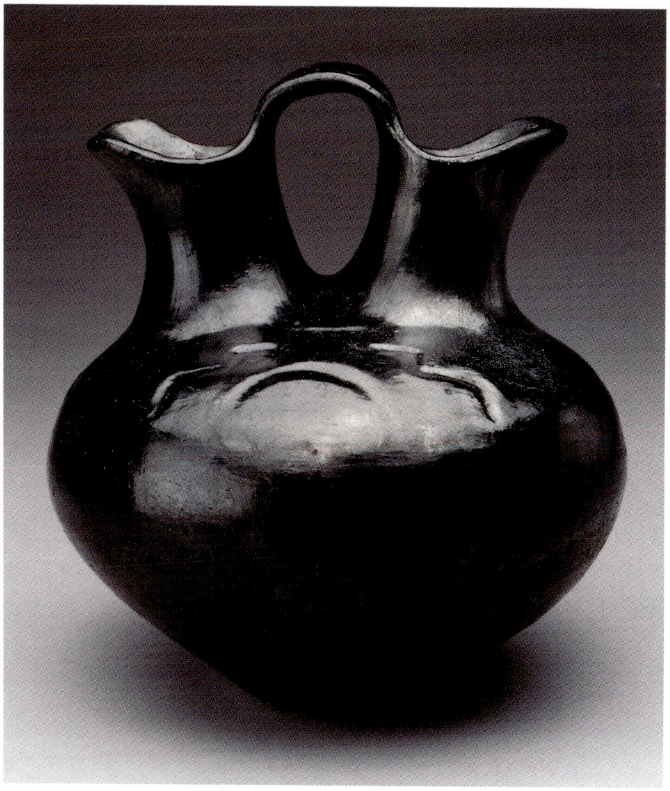

▶
49

Polished Blackware Wedding Vessel
ca. 1930
Height: 10″

Gift of
Amelia Elizabeth White

1937.530

can be very elaborate. Frequently stepped designs and others such as the avanyu, or water serpent, are carved in a framed area that might encircle the entire vessel.

TODAY, SOME POTTERS AT SANTA CLARA work with the clay in a manner that is quite contemporary while at the same time acknowledging the established tradition. Many potters, however, continue to work in a more traditional manner. Lu Ann Tafoya is a member of one of the most active and influential families of Santa Clara potters. Her elegant works are highly polished and are as successful as sculptural forms as they are pottery vessels (fig. 56). Distantly related to the Tafoya family is Linda Cain who creates traditional forms such as water jars with carved decoration (fig. 54). One of Linda's daughters is Autumn Borts, who prefers to create the cylindrical jar forms that are typical of Santa Clara pottery (fig. 53). Another outstanding Santa Clara potter is Virginia Garcia, who specializes in creating vessels with gracefully rounded features similar to the forms produced at Santa Clara over a century ago (fig. 55).

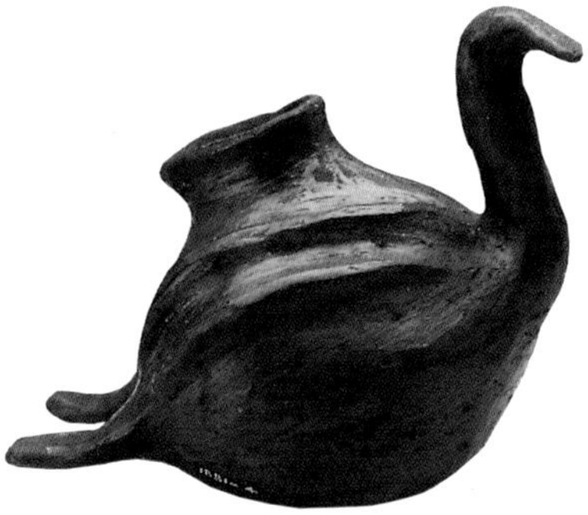

◀
50

POLISHED BLACKWARE
BIRD EFFIGY VESSEL
ca. 1880
Height: 5½″

Gift of Mrs. Larz Anderson

1881.4

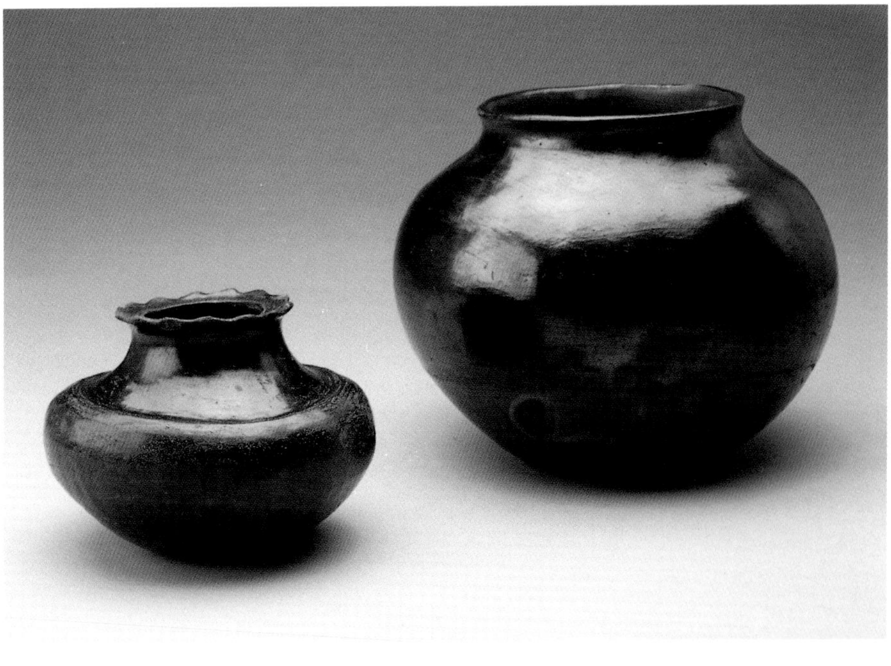

▶
51 *(left)*

POLISHED BLACKWARE JAR
ca. 1880
Height: 5½″

Collected by James Stevenson
Gift of the Women's Art Museum Association through exchange with the United States National Museum

1885.59

▶
52 *(right)*

POLISHED BLACKWARE JAR
ca. 1890
Height: 9½″

Gift of
General M. F. Force

1894.323

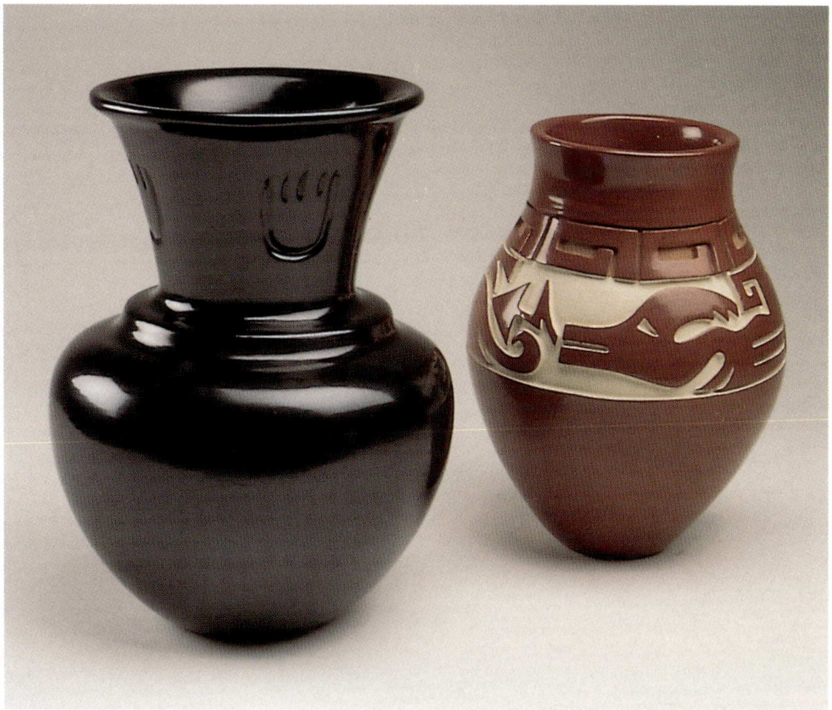

◀
53 *(left)*

Polished Blackware Jar
Autumn Borts
1994
Height: 11⅜″
....
Museum Purchase: Gift of Norman A. Murdock

1994.259

◀
54 *(right)*

Carved Redware Jar
Linda Cain
1994
Height: 10″
....
Museum Purchase: Gift of Alex and Joan Keller; Bill and Pam Koenig

1994.260

55 *(left)* ▶

Polished Blackware Jar
Virginia Garcia
1994
Height: 12⅜″
....
Museum Purchase: Gift of Roger and Pat Fry

1994.258

56 *(right)* ▶

Polished Blackware Jar
Lu Ann Tafoya
1994
Height: 13⅝″
....
Museum Purchase: Gift of Manuel D. and Rhoda Mayerson Foundation; Thomas R. Schiff

1994.257

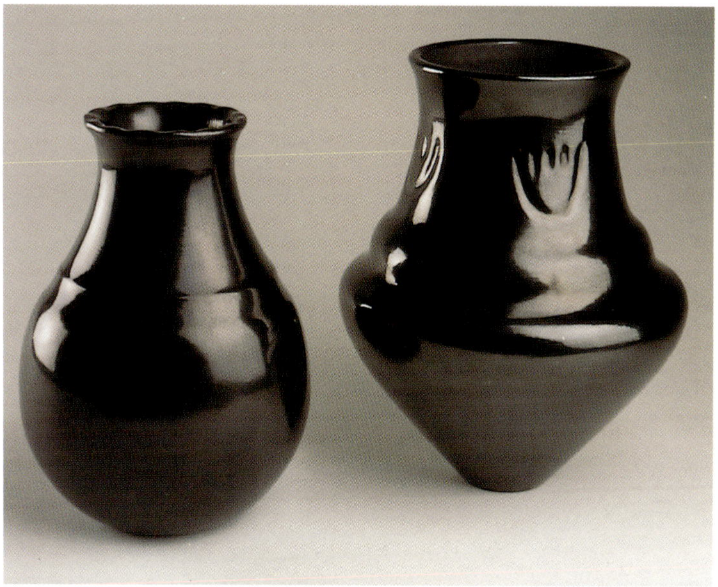

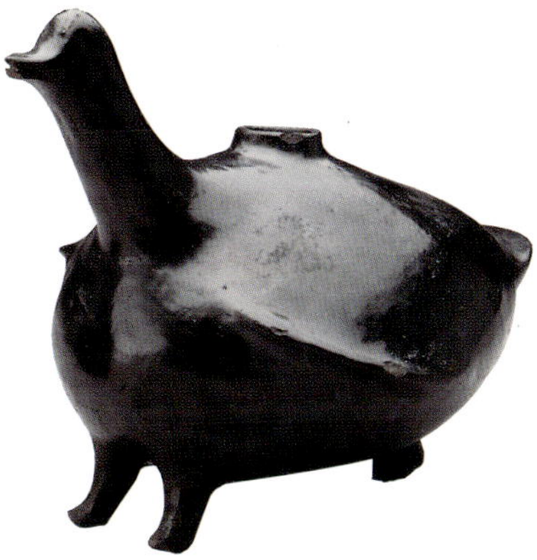

◀
57

Polished Blackware Bird Effigy Vessel
ca. 1880
Height: 7½″
....
Gift of Denver and Rio Grande Railroad

1886.17

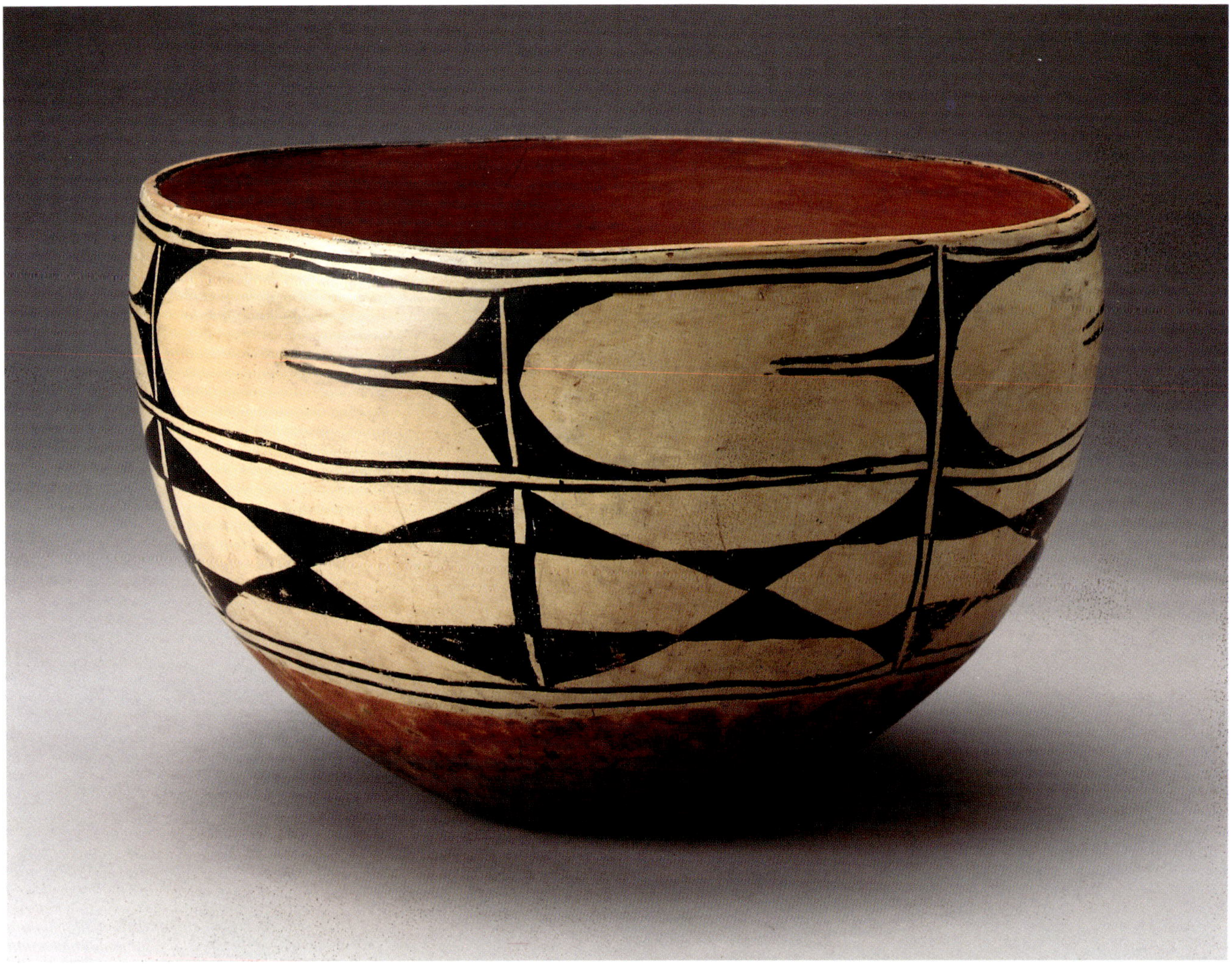

▲
58

Polychrome Bowl
ca. 1880
Diameter: 16″

Gift of Amelia Elizabeth White

1937.385

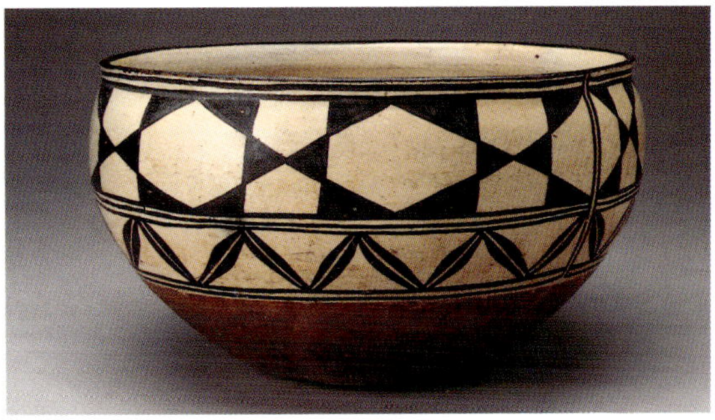

◀
59

Polychrome Bowl
ca. 1900
Diameter: 17¾″

Gift of Amelia Elizabeth White

1937.513

Santo Domingo

Santo Domingo Pueblo is often regarded as one of the more culturally conservative of the pueblos. That conservatism is reflected in the traditional style of Santo Domingo pottery, which has changed very little over the past two centuries. The most common pottery forms created at Santo Domingo are jars and bowls. The jars are generally more cylindrically shaped than the jar forms made at Acoma, Laguna, or Zia. Another unique feature is that Santo Domingo potters tend to give their jars flaring rims. The other common Santo Domingo pottery form is a bowl. Bowls are constructed with thick walls and have flat bottoms. The largest Santo Domingo bowls are frequently much larger than the bowls produced at any other pueblo (figs. 58, 59). It is not uncommon for older Santo Domingo "dough bowls" to be more than twenty inches in diameter and weigh more than ten pounds.

The decoration on most Santo Domingo pottery begins with a cream-colored slip and a red slip underbody, although black-on-red and polychrome vessels with black and red designs on a cream slip are not uncommon. The painted designs are then placed within a framed horizontal band on the exterior of bowls, just below the rim. The interiors of bowls are

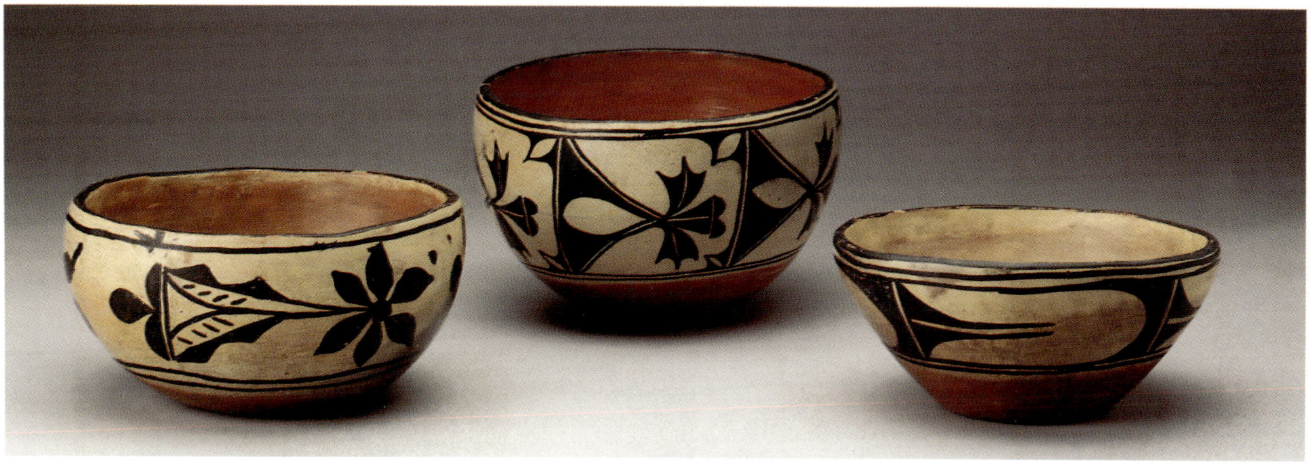

▲
60

Polychrome Bowl
ca. 1940
Diameter: 9″

Museum Purchase: Gift of Mrs. Hugh Smythe and Rebecca Scarborough, by exchange

1994.36

▲
61

Polychrome Bowl
ca. 1930
Diameter: 9¼″

Gift of Amelia Elizabeth White

1937.378

▲
62

Polychrome Bowl
ca. 1940
Diameter: 8¾″

Museum Purchase: Various Deaccession Funds

1994.32

also sometimes painted with an isolated design located in the center. On jars, the horizontal band containing the design elements is focused around the midsection of the vessel.

TODAY, SANTO DOMINGO POTTERS continue to use the same design elements that have been painted on vessels for the last two hundred years. These designs are often based on simple geometric forms, such as triangles (fig. 64), and are remarkably bold. Frequently, the design is arrived at by painting an area in black and allowing the cream slip to reveal the desired motif, thus creating a "negative" design. In addition to the bold geometric designs, floral and bird motifs are also sometimes painted. Another unique feature of Santo Domingo pottery is that the painted design on each vessel has a break in it called the Spirit Path. The Spirit Path, or Line Break, can be traced back to prehistoric pottery in the Southwest and is a symbolic device. It is believed that the interruption of the design provides an outlet to prevent the spirit of the vessel from being trapped within the design (Chapman, 1977:35-36). Currently at Santo Domingo, there are potters who continue to base their work on the traditional forms and painted designs. The most well known and prolific of these potters are Robert Tenorio (fig. 63) and his family: his sister Hilda and her husband, Arthur Coriz (fig. 64). They all produce and sell their pottery in a workshop-like atmosphere involving the entire extended family in the process. Also at Santo Domingo are other potters such as Petra Garcia, who continues in the pueblo's tradition of creating the monumental dough bowls (fig. 65).

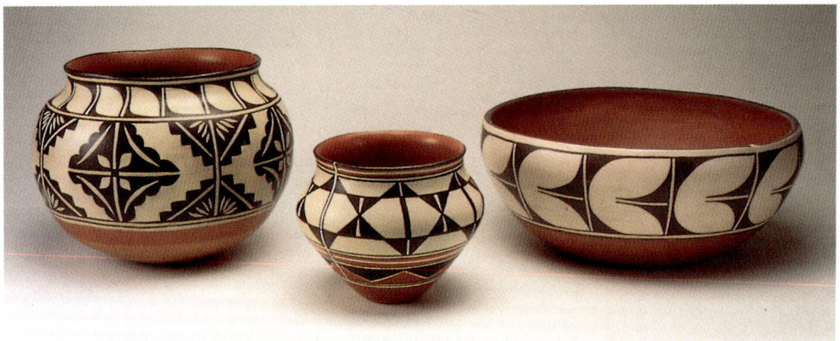

▲ 63 *(left)*

POLYCHROME JAR
ROBERT TENORIO
ca. 1992
Height: 13⅛″

Museum Purchase: Gift of
Roger and Pat Fry

1994.125

◀ 64 *(center)*

POLYCHROME JAR
ARTHUR & HILDA CORIZ
1994
Diameter: 9¼″

Gift of
Mr. and Mrs. J. Dwight Thompson

1994.124

◀ 65 *(right)*

POLYCHROME BOWL
PETRA GARCIA
1994
Diameter: 21⅜″

Gift of Gail and Fred Berger

1994.261

66 *(left)* ▶

POLYCHROME JAR
ca. 1930
Height: 10¼″

Gift of
Amelia Elizabeth White

1937.380

67 *(right)* ▶

BLACK-ON-RED JAR
ca. 1930
Height: 10¾″

Gift of
Amelia Elizabeth White

1937.519

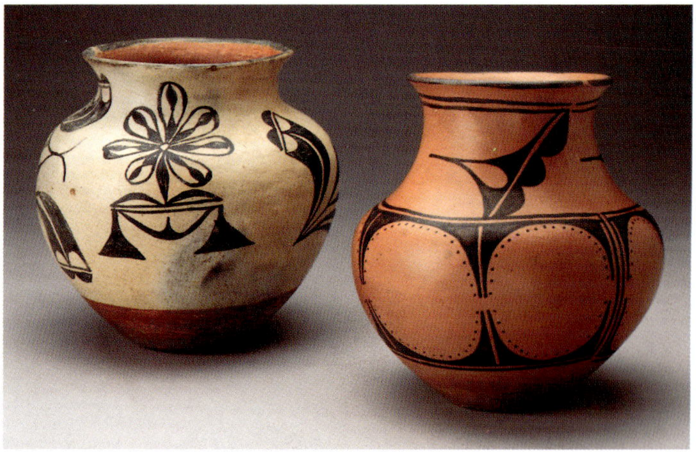

Taos and Picuris

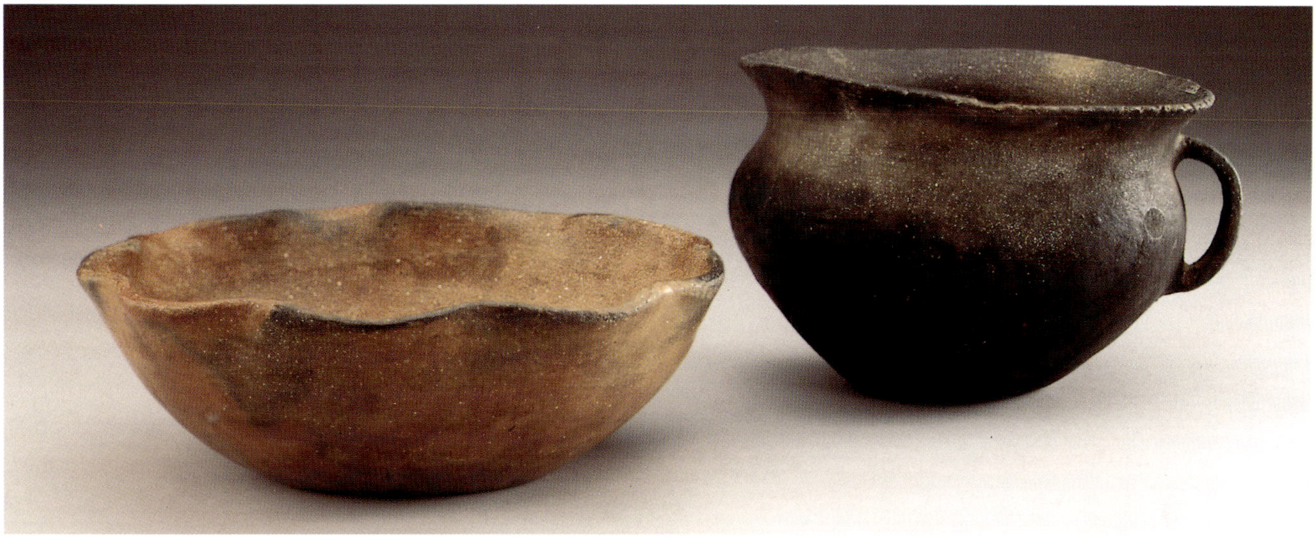

▲
68

Micaceous Bowl
ca. 1930
Diameter: 9½″

Museum Purchase:
Gift of Dr. and Mrs. Sanford R. Courter

1991.177

▲
69

Micaceous Bean Pot
ca. 1920
Height: 5½″

Museum Purchase:
Various Deaccession Funds

1994.37

While pottery made with micaceous clay is characteristic of the northern Rio Grande pueblos as well as the Jicarilla Apache, it is perhaps best known from Taos and nearby Picuris pueblos. Historically, micaceous vessels produced at these two pueblos are virtually indistinguishable.

Micaceous clay glitters in its natural state consisting as it does of eroded pre-Cambrian schist filled with flecks of mica. The mica inclusions function as a temper: no additional temper is required. After firing, the clay has a sparkling, orange-brown appearance often marked by black fire clouds. The fire clouds

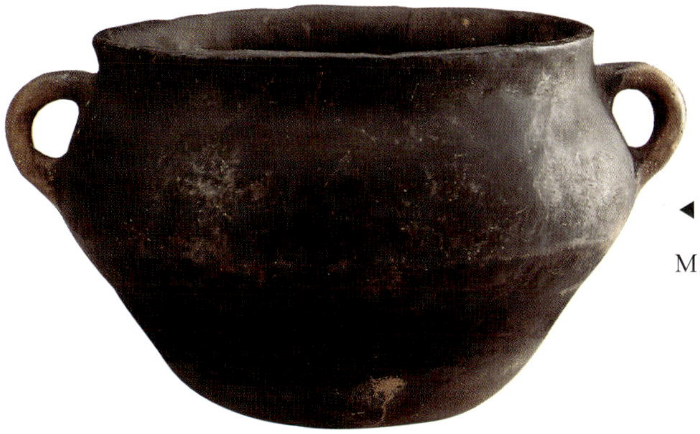

◀ 70

Micaceous Bean Pot
ca. 1900
Height: 5½″

Museum Purchase:
Gift of Dr. and Mrs. Sanford R. Courter

1991.176

are considered to be aesthetically pleasing and part of the overall style.

MICACEOUS POTTERY FROM TAOS AND PICURIS are unslipped and unpainted. In describing her pottery, Virginia Romero of Taos states, "I just shape them and smooth them; I don't polish them. I scrape them with a file. I just file them and then I make them smooth with my hand. That's all." (Trimble, 1987:33). Because there is no painted decoration on micaceous pottery, the emphasis is on creating expressive forms. The most common forms are tall, round-bottomed jars and shorter globular jars with flared rims. The shorter, more rounded forms, known as bean pots, have one or two handles (fig. 70) and often have lids as well. The name for this form is in reference to its primary use as a cooking vessel. It is a traditional form that was used not only by pueblo people but also by the Hispanic people in the surrounding area. The functional aspect of the bean pots is further emphasized by the darkened surfaces that result from being placed directly on a cooking fire time and time again.

FOR THE PAST CENTURY, few micaceous pottery pieces other than bean pots have been created. Micaceous pottery was never as commercially successful as the painted pottery produced at some of the other pueblos. Currently, however, a renaissance in making pottery using micaceous clay is underway, and younger potters such as Rita Donna Martinez (fig. 72) and Annette Duran (fig.71), both from Taos Pueblo, have turned to working with the clay. Anthony Durand is perhaps the best-known potter from Picuris. His distinctive vessels (fig. 73) are unique for their highly polished surfaces and their silver color, the result of using a specific type of micaceous clay that fires silver rather than orange.

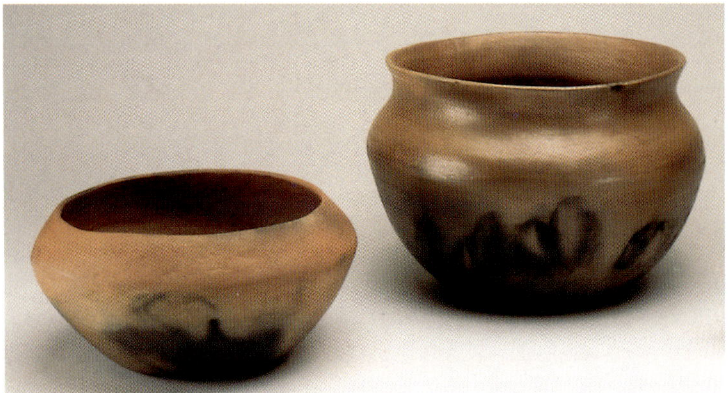

▲
71

MICACEOUS BOWL
ANNETTE DURAN
1994
Diameter: 12"

Museum Purchase: Gift of
Dr. and Mrs. Sanford R. Courter

1994.263

▲
72

MICACEOUS JAR
RITA DONNA MARTINEZ
1994
Height: 9¾"

Museum Purchase:
Gift of Myra and Louis Chabut

1994.262

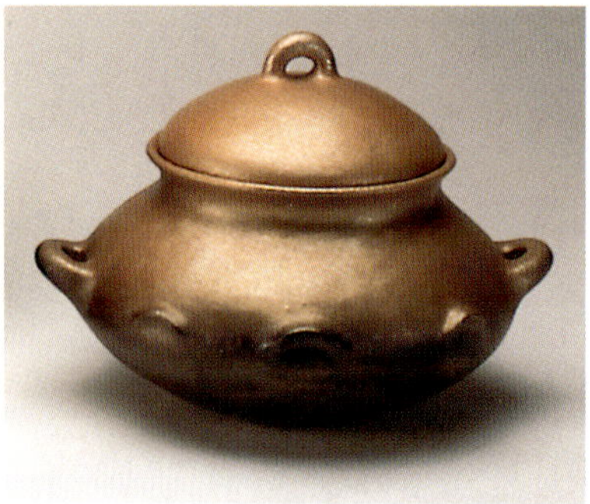

▲
73

MICACEOUS BEAN POT
ANTHONY DURAND
1994
Height: 8¼"

Museum Purchase: Gift of
Dr. and Mrs. Sanford R. Courter

1994.264

Tesuque

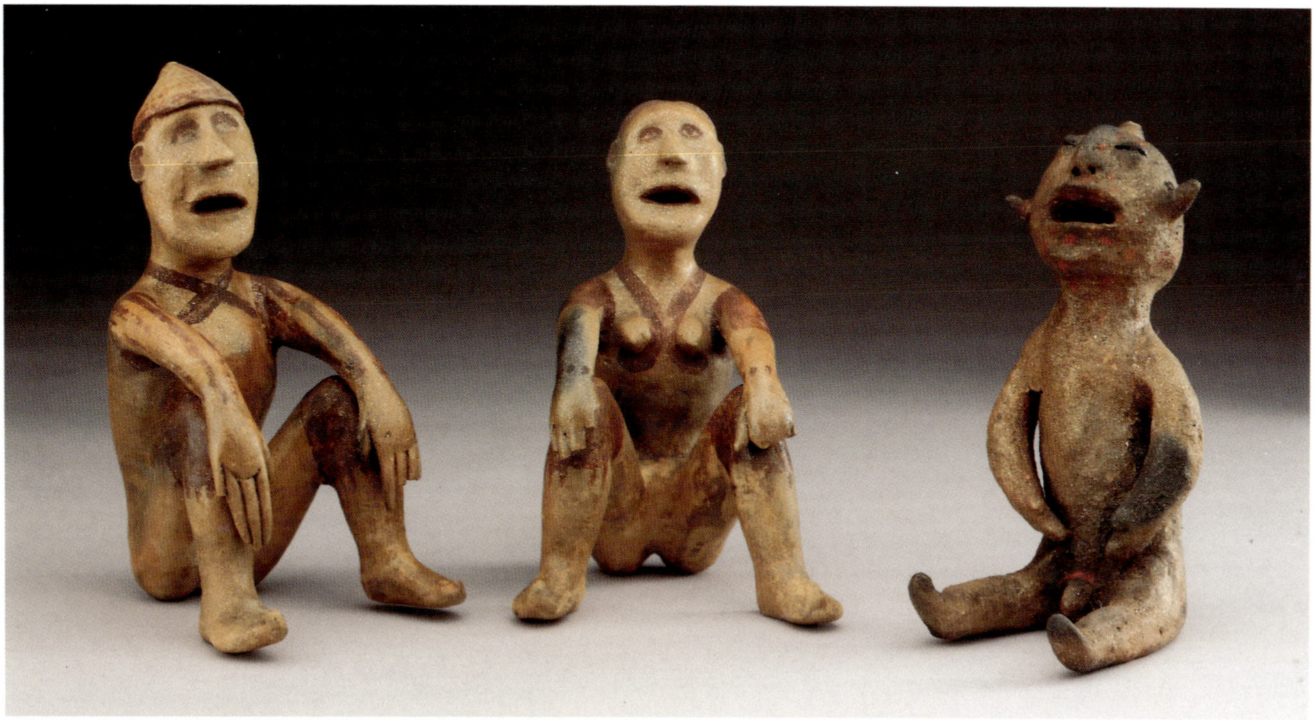

▲
74

Micaceous Figure
ca. 1880
Height: 8″

Gift of Denver and Rio Grande Railroad

1886.32

▲
75

Micaceous Figure
ca. 1880
Height: 7¾″

Gift of Denver and Rio Grande Railroad

1886.31

▲
76

Micaceous Figure
ca.1880
Height: 7½

Gift of Mrs. Daniel H. Farny in memory of Daniel H. Farny

1986.1040

The pottery of Tesuque Pueblo has undergone a tremendous amount of change resulting in a variety of styles and forms. At the middle of the nineteenth century, most traditional Tesuque pottery was decorated with complex motifs loosely painted in black on a white slip with a red slip underbody. In many instances these vessels are stylistically similar to those produced at Cochiti Pueblo, Tesuque's closest neighbor to the south. However, unique to Tesuque pottery is an interlocking fret design that was commonly painted on bowls (fig.77). In addition to vessels with black-on-white designs, a small number of black-on-red vessels similar to those from nearby San Ildefonso Pueblo were created (fig. 81), as well as a full range of utilitarian vessels, such

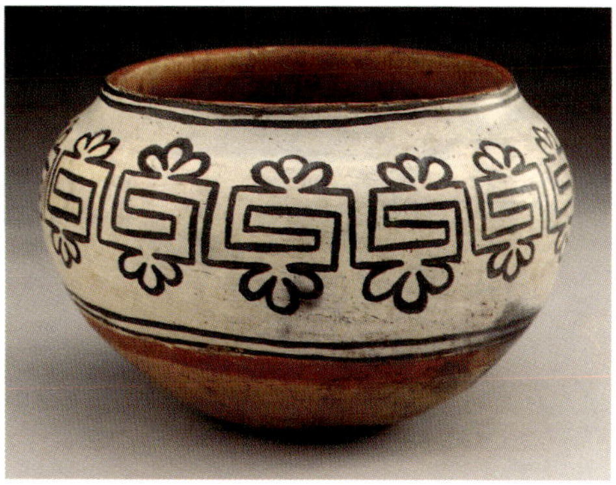

◀
77

Polychrome Jar
ca. 1880
Height: 6½″

Museum Appropriation

x-1994.2

as bean pots made from micaceous clay.

TOWARD THE END of the nineteenth century, at the urging of traders in Santa Fe, Tesuque potters began to create a variety of forms in order to respond to the increasing demands of tourists and the mail-order market. Pitchers and small flowerpots with drainholes in the bottom were produced and painted with typical Tesuque floral designs. However, the most characteristic form of Tesuque pottery by the turn of the century were the small figures known as Rain Gods. These are seated human figures, often female, posed with their legs straight out and holding a small jar. These figures appear to have been first developed around 1879; early examples are often made with micaceous clay and posed with bent legs (figs. 74-76). However, these micaceous figures were quickly replaced by small non-micaceous figures that were highlighted with bright poster paints after being fired. Currently, there are very few potters who are creating traditional style Tesuque vessels. Most, like Ignacia Duran, work with micaceous clay. Her recent work includes very light weight, thin walled bowls (fig. 80) as well as wonderfully detailed Rain Gods (fig. 79). Priscilla Vigil is another Tesuque potter who specializes in creating utilitarian forms, such as bean pots (fig. 82), in addition to the more commercially oriented Rain Gods.

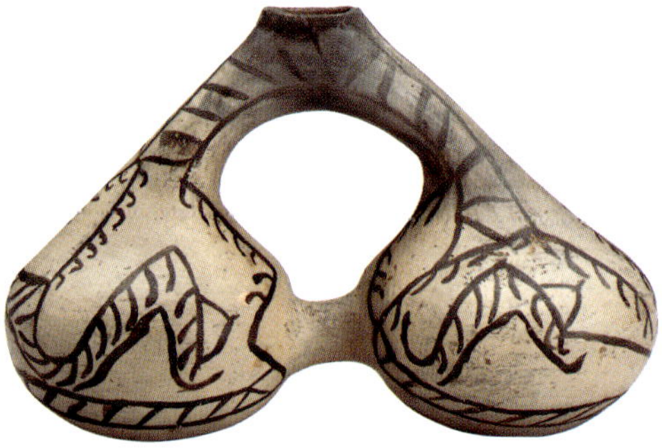

▲
78

BLACK-ON-WHITE BI-LOBED CANTEEN
ca. *1880*
Height: 6¼″
....
Gift of Denver and Rio Grande Railroad

1886.58

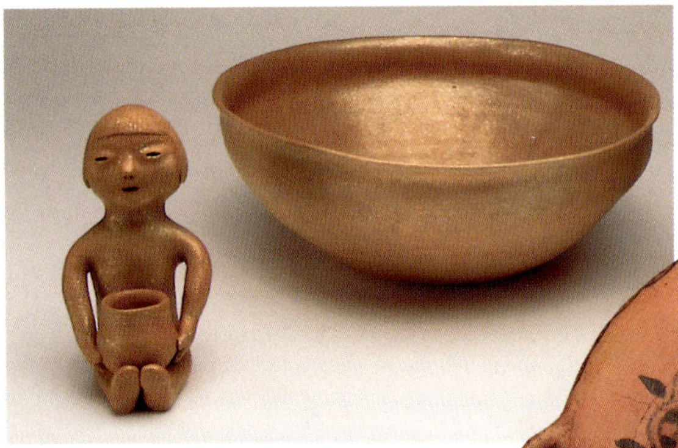

▲
79 *(left)*

MICACEOUS RAIN GOD
IGNACIA DURAN
1994
Height: 7″
....
Museum Purchase:
Gift of Roger and Pat Fry

1994.266

▲
80 *(right)*

MICACEOUS BOWL
IGNACIA DURAN
1986
Diameter: 14″
....
Museum Purchase:
Gift of Susan and Clinton Nagy;
Susan and Daniel Pfau

1994.265

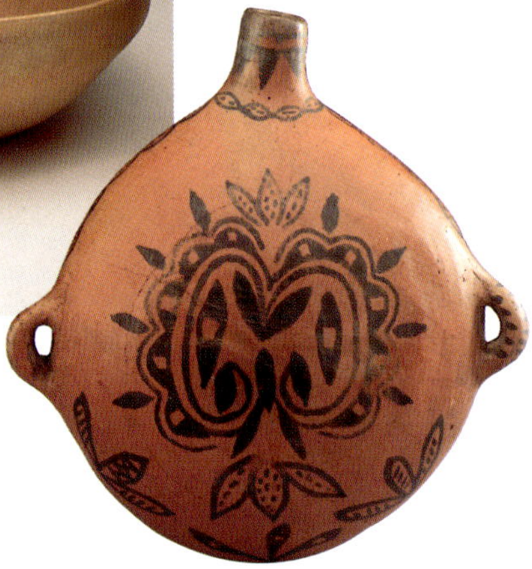

▲
81

BLACK-ON-RED CANTEEN
ca. 1880
Height: 11½″
....
Lent by Frank D. Goodhue

135.1890

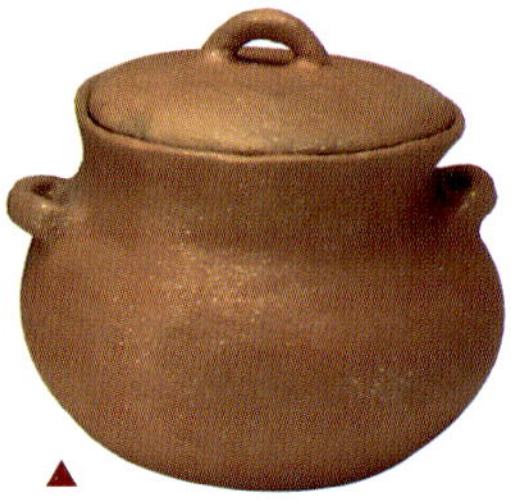

▲
82

MICACEOUS BEAN POT
PRISCILLA VIGIL
1994
Height: 8″
....
Museum Purchase:
Gift of
Valerie L. Newell

1994.267

ZIA

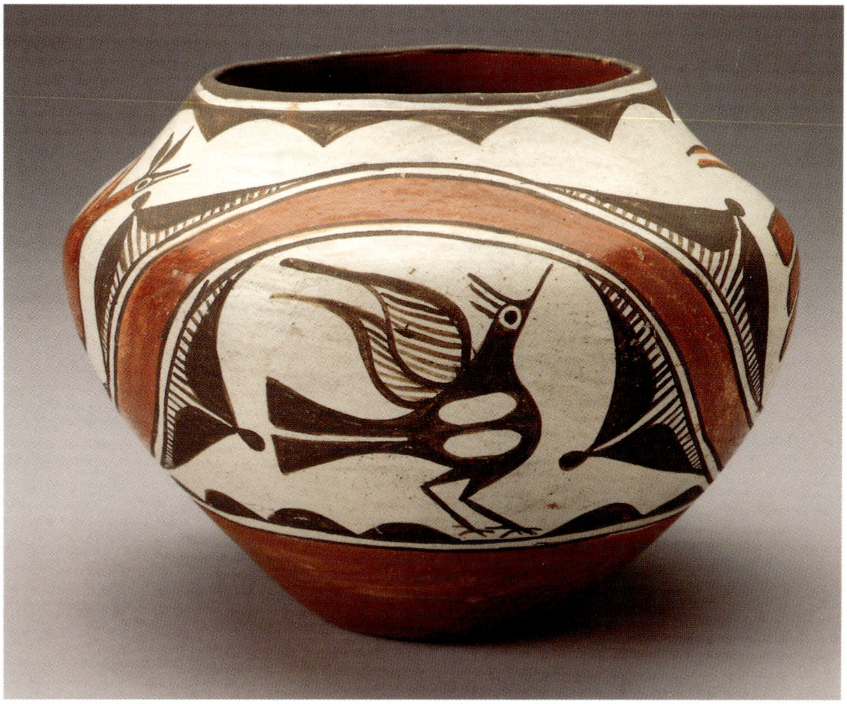

◄
83

POLYCHROME JAR
ca. 1950
Height: 8″

Museum Purchase:
Gift of Mr. and Mrs.
Clyde Abbot,
by exchange

1994.35

FOR MANY CENTURIES Zia Pueblo has been a center of pottery production. Historically, Zia pottery was traded for agricultural crops from Jemez and San Felipe pueblos to compensate for Zia's poor farmland. Traditional Zia pottery is made from a reddish clay with ground black basalt mixed as temper. The most common forms of Zia pottery are jars and bowls. Typically jars are often given a high shoulder, and extremely large examples of eighteen inches or more in height are not uncommon. Zia bowls have flat bottoms and are created in a variety of sizes with the largest rivaling the monumental dough bowls from Santo Domingo.

AFTER BEING FORMED, Zia vessels are usually coated with a white or buff-colored slip except for the underbody, which is often given a red slip to match that on the rim interiors of jars and the interiors of bowls. The designs painted on many Zia vessels are worked within a design field extending from the rim to the underbody. This area, which may or may not be further divided into registers, or panels, is always framed by a pair of parallel lines around the top of the underbody and either one or two lines around the rim.

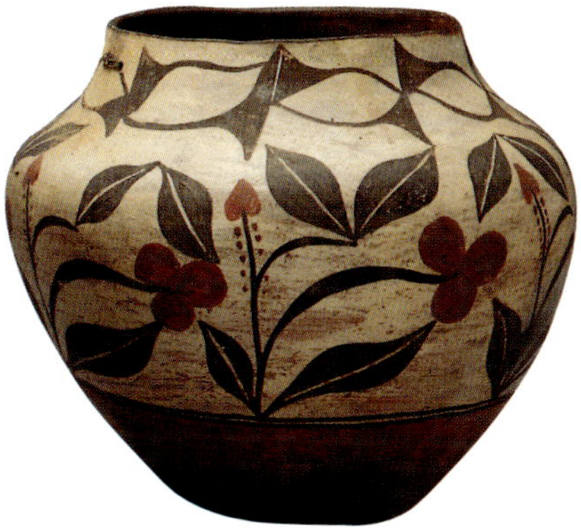

◄
84

POLYCHROME JAR
ca. 1900
Height: 10¾″

Gift of
Amelia Elizabeth White

1937.522

TRADITIONAL DESIGNS PAINTED ON ZIA pottery include bold geometric elements that are visually similar to those used by Acoma and Laguna potters (fig. 84). One of the most common of the geometric elements found on Zia pottery is a stepped design that represents clouds (fig. 88). However, the most characteristic motif on traditional Zia pottery is a distinctive style of bird that first became popular in the middle of the nineteenth century (fig. 83). The bird is depicted in profile with a single large eye and two feathers atop its head, a straight beak, and a long tail that may or may not be split. Potters identify this bird as a roadrunner which, to the Zia people, is a symbol of speed and a bearer of prayers. The roadrunner is frequently painted in association with a red or orange-and-red arc. This arc, representing the rainbow, serves as both a decorative and framing device. Other common design elements include abstract feathers, feathered prayer sticks, and plants.

CURRENTLY AT ZIA there are only a few potters who work in the traditional manner. Of these potters, the Medina family is particularly well known. Sofia Medina learned pottery-making from her mother-in-law, Trinidad Medina, who was famous for her

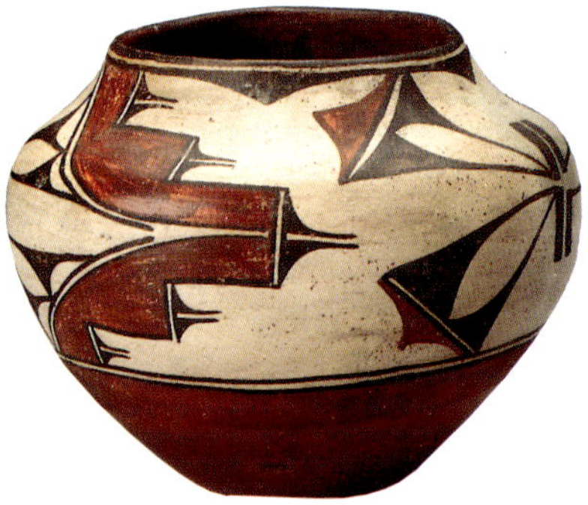

◀ 85

POLYCHROME JAR
ca. 1950
Height: 7½″

Museum Purchase:
Gift of Edward Greeno, Jr.
Mrs. Tyler Field
Mrs. Hugh Smythe
Rebecca Scarborough
by exchange

1994.38

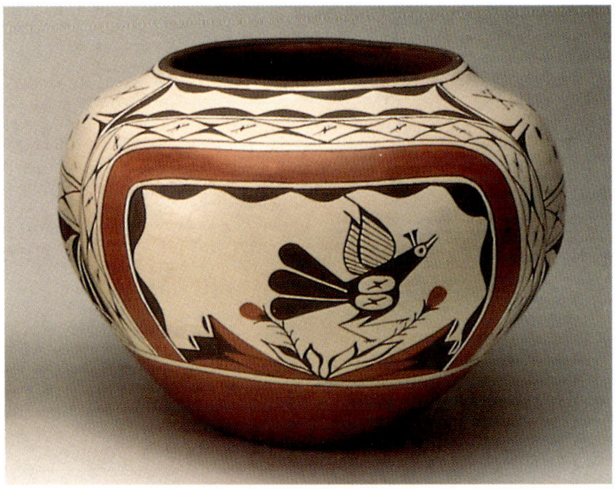

▲ 86

POLYCHROME JAR
KATHERINE PINO
1994
Height: 11½″

Museum Purchase:
Gift of
Judge & Mrs. Mark A. Painter;
Timothy A. Smith

1994.271

▼ 87

POLYCHROME JAR
KATHERINE PINO
1994
Height: 11½″

Museum Purchase:
Gift of Myra and Louis Chabut

1994.270

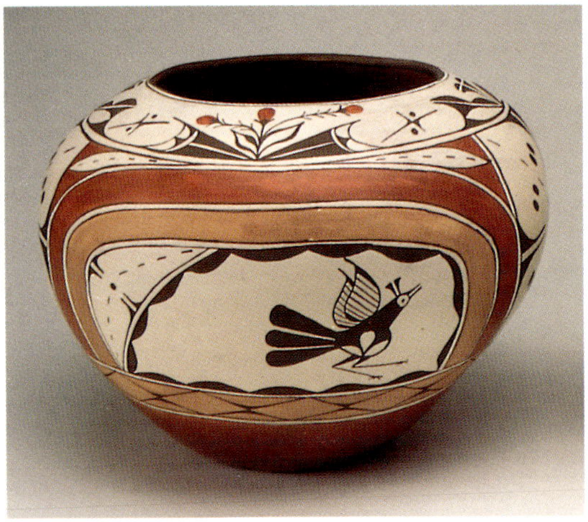

▶ 88

POLYCHROME BOWL
ca. 1950
Diameter: 9″

Museum Purchase:
Various Deaccession Funds

1994.33

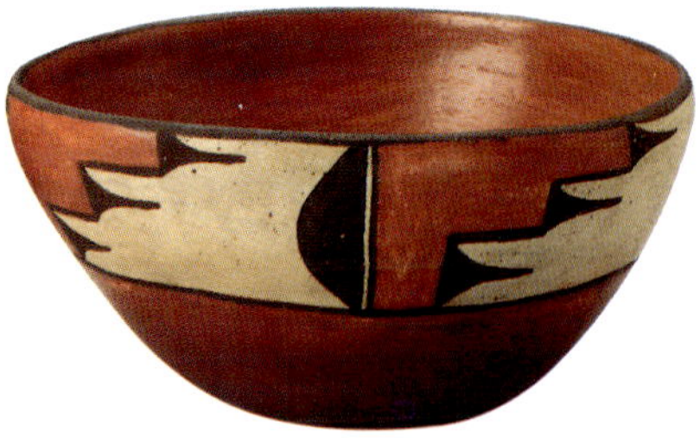

huge storage jars painted with traditional Zia designs. In turn, Sofia Medina has taught her children to create traditional Zia vessels. She and her daughter Lois are especially renowned for their ability to create large vessels as well as reviving the buff-colored slip, a Medina family trademark (figs. 89, 91). Other traditional potters at Zia, like Katherine Pino and her niece Reyes Pino, who paints the pottery her aunt makes, prefer the distinctive Zia designs on white-slipped vessels (figs. 86, 87).

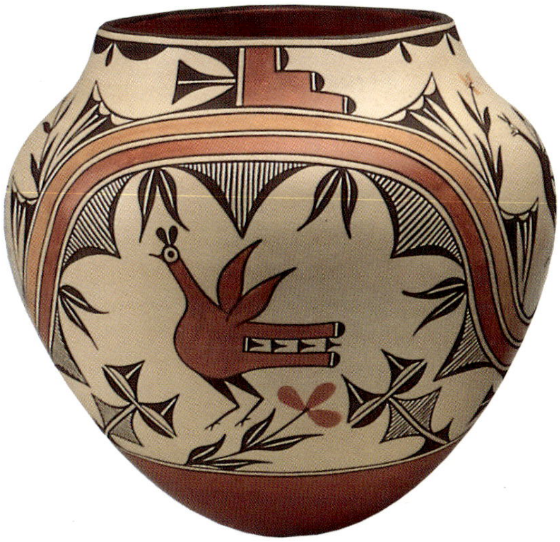

▲
89

POLYCHROME JAR
SOFIA MEDINA
1994
Height: 17″

Museum Purchase: Gift of
Manuel D. and Rhoda Mayerson Foundation;
Gretchen B. McCormick

1994.268

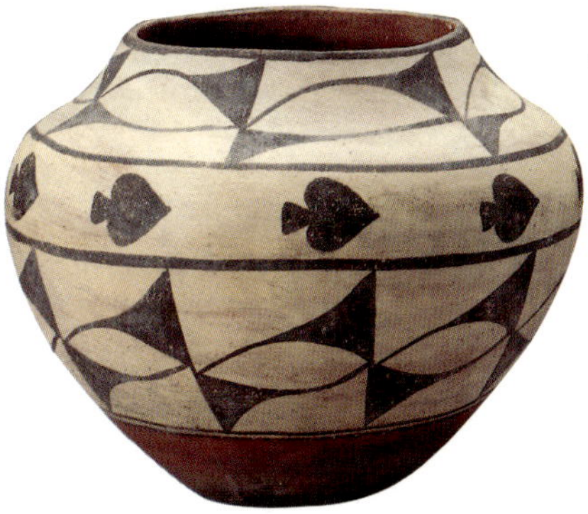

◀ 90

POLYCHROME JAR
ca. 1930
Height: 8¾″

Gift of
Amelia Elizabeth White

1937.517

▼
91

POLYCHROME BOWL
LOIS MEDINA
1994
Diameter: 18⅝″

Museum Purchase:
Gift of Gail and Fred Berger;
Thomas R. Schiff

1994.269

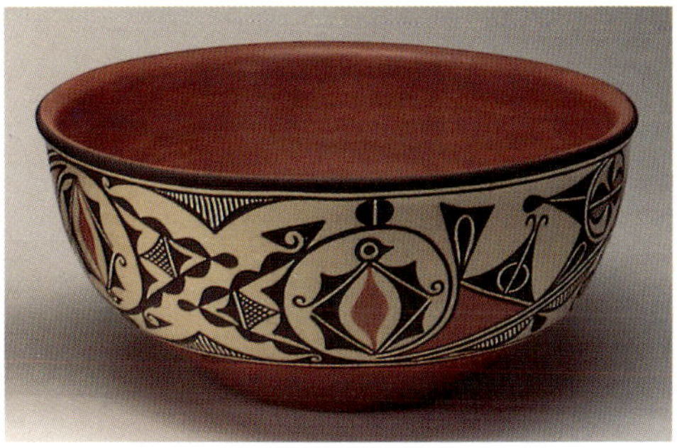

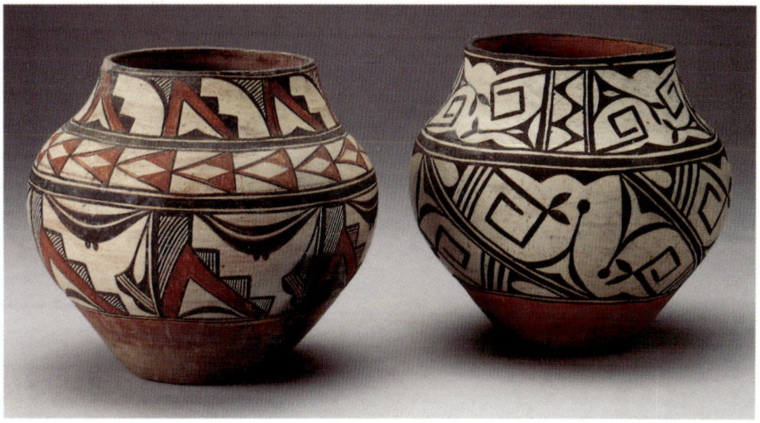

▲
92

POLYCHROME JAR
ca. 1930
Height: 8¾″

Gift of
Amelia Elizabeth White

1937.521

▲
93

POLYCHROME JAR
ca. 1930
Height: 9″

Gift of
Amelia Elizabeth White

1937.516

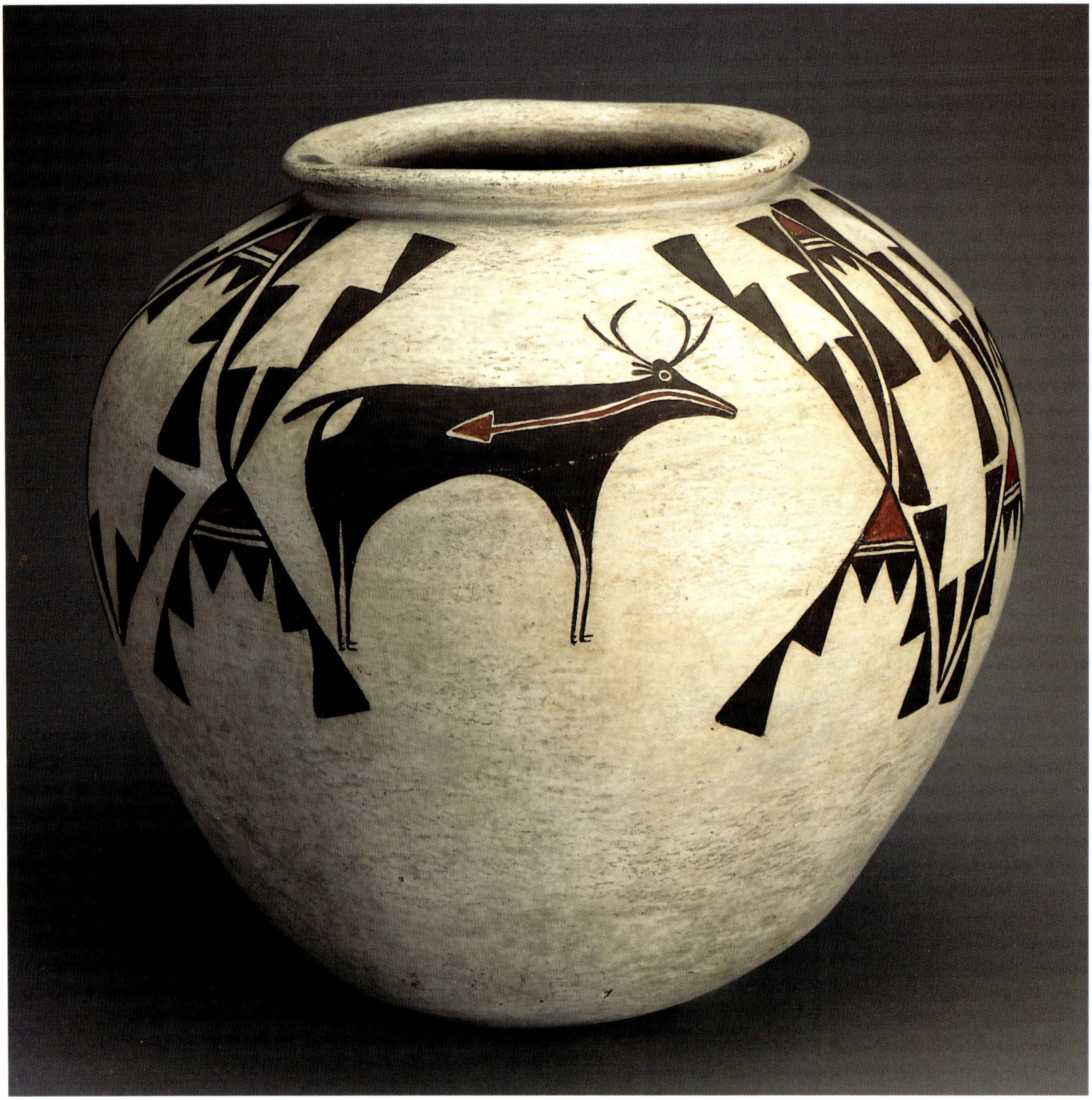

▲
94

Polychrome Drum
Tsayutitsa(?)
ca. 1930
Height: 20½″
....
Gift of
Amelia Elizabeth White

1937.528

▶
95

Polychrome Bowl
ca. 1880
Diameter: 12¾″
....
Collected by James Stevenson
Gift of the Women's Art Museum
Association through exchange with
the United States National Museum

1885.71

ZUNI

HISTORICALLY, ZUNI POTTERY IS MADE from locally collected gray-white clay and then mixed with crushed potsherds for temper. There are a variety of forms, with the most numerous being jars and bowls. The most common jar is a high-shouldered form. Sometimes the transition from the shoulder to the neck is pronounced, while at other times there is a more subtle transition. Drums are a specific type of jar. They are large jars with thick walls and have sharply everted rims to allow a skin to be stretched over the mouth for use as a drumhead (fig. 94). Zuni bowls characteristically have a slight constriction below a flaring rim. One specialized type of bowl has stepped sides and may have a strap handle. These are called cornmeal bowls by the Zuni people. These bowls are used to carry cornmeal in ceremonies (figs. 97, 104). After the ceremonies are completed they are returned to the maker and frequently sold.

MOST ZUNI POTTERY IS DECORATED with polychrome designs painted on a white slip. The design layout on Zuni vessels is fairly standard. On jars, the design may be an overall pattern or may be divided into two or three registers on the body, with a completely different design painted on the neck (fig. 98). On bowls, there is usually an overall design on the interior with a separate design around the inside of the rim (fig. 95). On the exterior, repeated designs encircle the bowl in a continuous pattern. Isolated designs are usually painted on cornmeal bowls that refer to water symbolism such as tadpoles, frogs, dragonflies, and butterflies. Traditional Zuni polychrome designs are usually painted in black and shades of brown, while red is used sparingly. Popular designs include geometric and spiral motifs. The deer, also sometimes referred to as an antelope, with a heart line is also frequently depicted by Zuni potters (fig. 94). In describ-

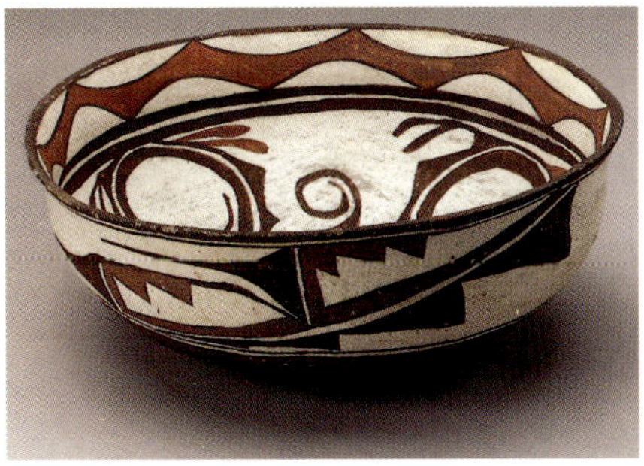

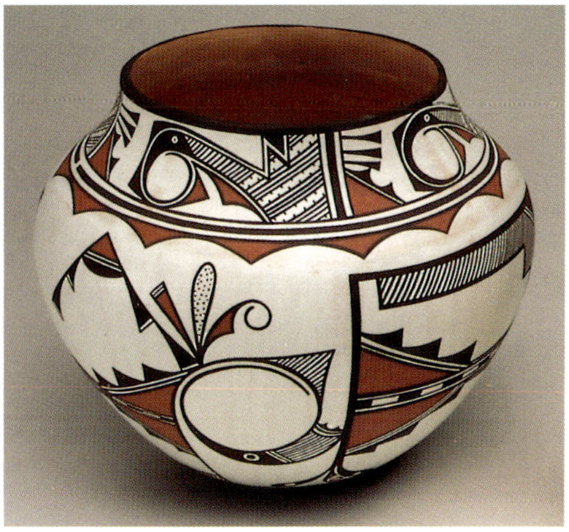

▶
96

POLYCHROME JAR
GABRIEL PALOMA
1994
Height: 9¼″

Museum Purchase:
Gift of
Mrs. Daniel S. Campbell

1994.274

ing this design it has been written: "The line running down from the animal's mouth and terminating at its heart may be described as a prayer. It is a pictographic invocation to the spirit of the antelope to incline the hearts of the antelope on earth to put themselves in the way of the Zunis that they may kill them for food." (Bloom 1933-1938, IX:199). Often the deer will be framed which is considered to be a traditional Zuni design known as "Deer in His House."

ANOTHER TRADITIONAL DESIGN that is referred to by name is the Rainbird. It is an all-over geometric design outlined in thick, dark lines and filled in with thin, fine-line hatching that symbolizes rain (fig. 102). The more naturalistic birds painted on traditional Zuni pottery are rather squat with long tails; they are often depicted with their beak touching a stylized flower (fig. 107). Rosettes, or medallions, are also a frequently used motif (figs. 99, 105). They are usually black with varying amounts of red added. This distinctive motif,

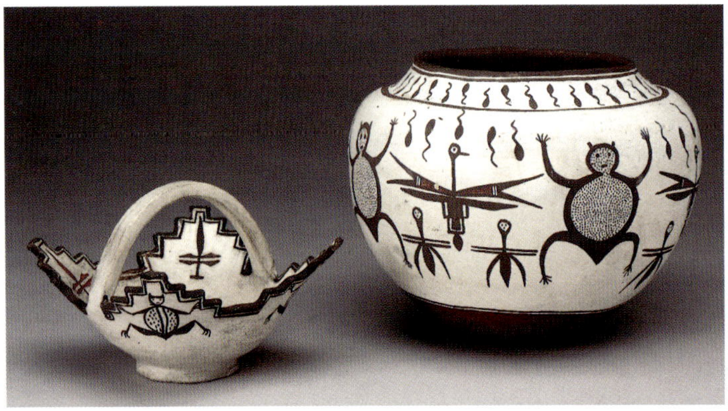

▲
97

POLYCHROME CORNMEAL BOWL
ca. 1880
Diameter: 9¾"

Collected by James Stevenson
Gift of the Women's Art Museum Association through exchange with the United States National Museum

1885.76

▲
98
POLYCHROME JAR
LENA ZUNI
1933
Height: 10"

Gift of Dr. Daniel Cook

1943.931

▼
99

POLYCHROME JAR
ca. 1940
Height: 19"

Gift of
Dr. Daniel Cook

1943.930

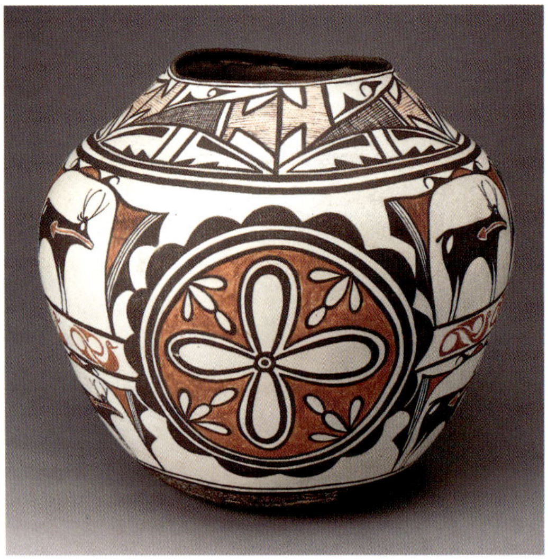

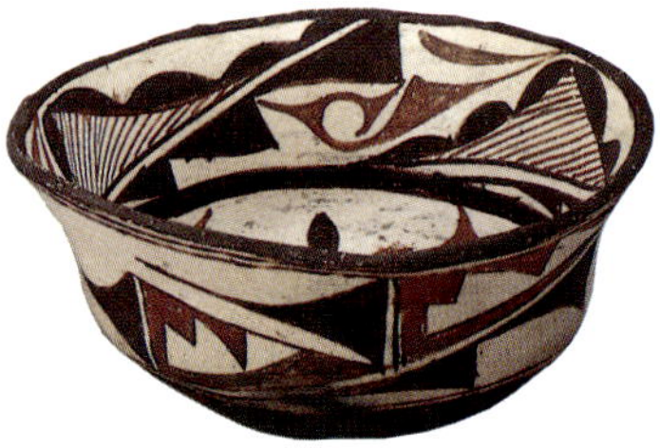

◀
100

POLYCHROME BOWL
ca. 1880
Diameter: 9½"

Collected by
James Stevenson
Gift of the Women's Art
Museum Association
through exchange with
the United States
National Museum

1885.88

▼
101

POLYCHROME BOWL
ca. 1880
Diameter: 14¾"

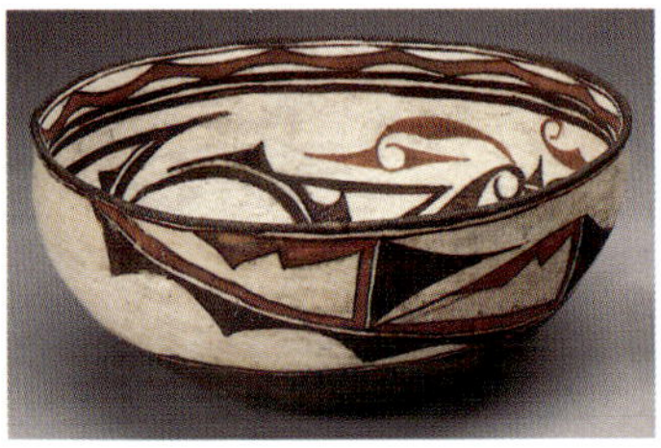

Collected by
James Stevenson
Gift of the Women's Art
Museum Association
through exchange with
the United States
National Museum

1885.70

likely of Hispanic influence, first appeared on Zuni jars in the late nineteenth century.

For many years traditional pottery-making at Zuni was waning, but now there are several potters who work in the traditional manner. One such potter is Gabriel Paloma (fig. 96), who first learned traditional pottery-making through a class at Zuni High School, where he now teaches that same subject. His

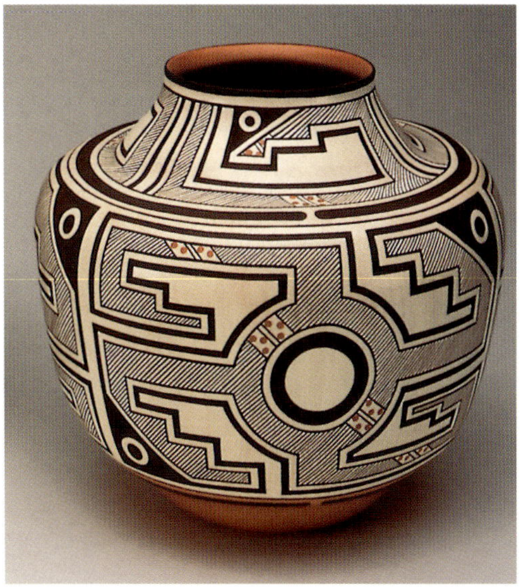

▲
102

Polychrome Jar
Randy Nahohai
1994
Height: 9¾″

Museum Purchase:
Gift of Lauren A. Schiff

1994.272

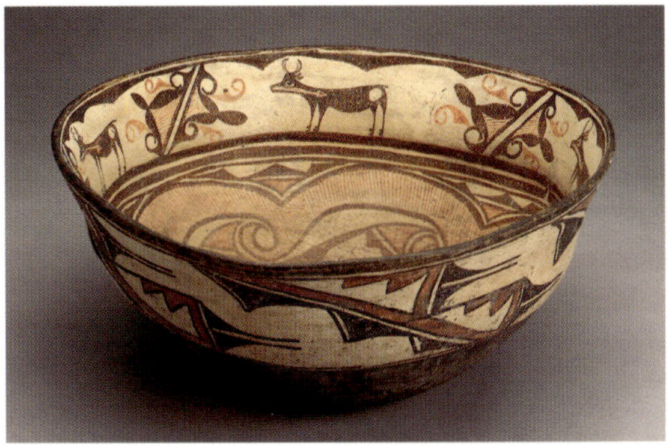

▲
103

Polychrome Bowl
ca. 1880
Diameter: 18¾″

Gift of Amelia Elizabeth White

1937.512

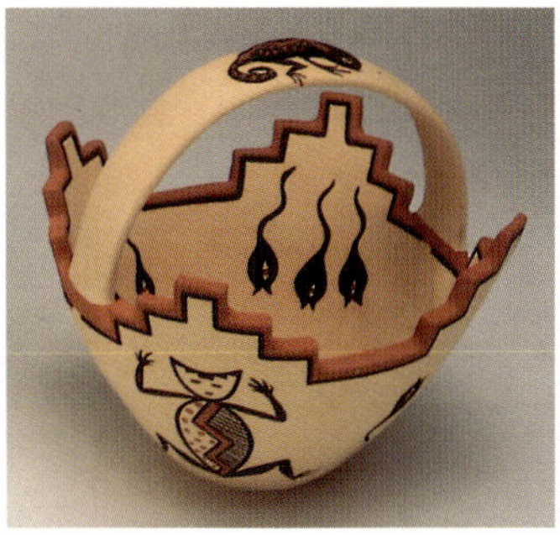

◀
104

Polychrome Cornmeal Bowl
Brenda Paloma
1994
Height: 6¾″

Museum Purchase:
Gift of
Mr. and Mrs. James J. Crowe

1994.275

▼
105 *(left)*

Polychrome Jar
ca. 1930
Height: 13″

Gift of Amelia Elizabeth White

1937.383

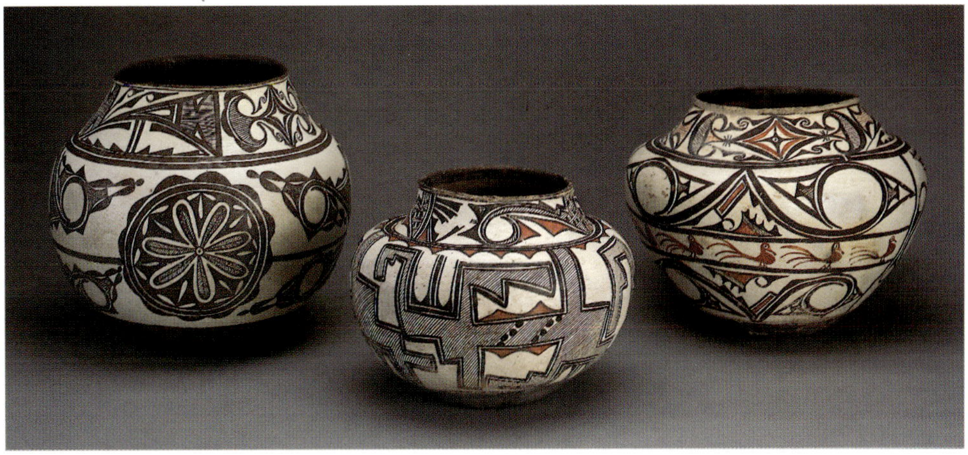

◀ 106 *(center)*

Polychrome Jar
ca. 1930
Height: 9″

Gift of Amelia Elizabeth White

1937.524

◀ 107 *(right)*

Polychrome Jar
ca. 1930
Height: 11½″

Gift of Amelia Elizabeth White

1937.384

sister, Brenda Paloma, is another traditional potter. Occasionally she prefers to leave her vessels unslipped because she likes the natural color of the clay when it is fired (fig. 104). Like the Palomas, Anderson Peynetsa is also quite active in creating pottery that refers to traditional Zuni forms and designs (fig. 108). One of the best known of the current Zuni potters is Randy Nahohai, who learned traditional techniques from his mother, Josephine, but who also studied graphic art at the Institute of American Indian Art in Santa Fe, New Mexico. Nahohai considers himself primarily a graphic artist who combines that talent with the inspiration he finds in the historic and prehistoric Zuni pottery in order to create dynamic traditionally styled vessels (fig. 102).

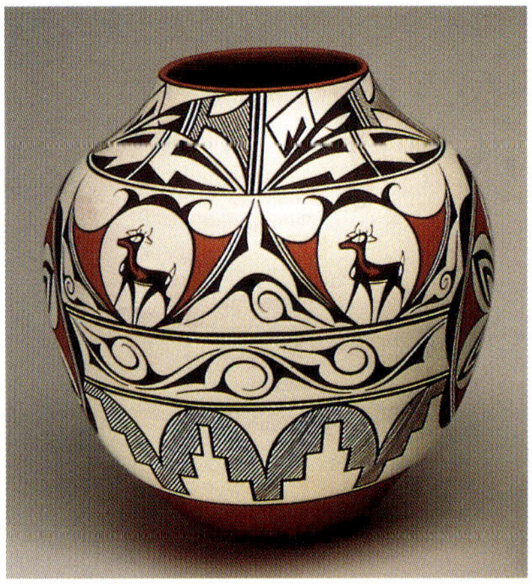

◀ 108

POLYCHROME JAR
ANDERSON PEYNETSA
1994
Height: 11″

Museum Purchase:
Gift of Gail and Fred Berger;
Miss Hillary Thompson

1994.273

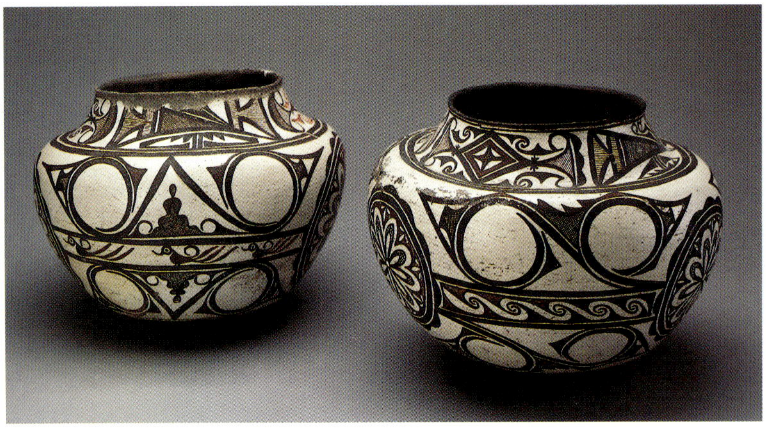

◀ 110

POLYCHROME JAR
ca. 1880
Height: 11¼″

Collected by
James Stevenson
Gift of the Women's Art
Museum Association
through exchange with
the United States
National Museum

1885.90

▲ 109

POLYCHROME JAR
ca. 1870
Height: 11½″

Collected by
James Stevenson
Gift of the Women's Art
Museum Association
through exchange with
the United States
National Museum

1885.49

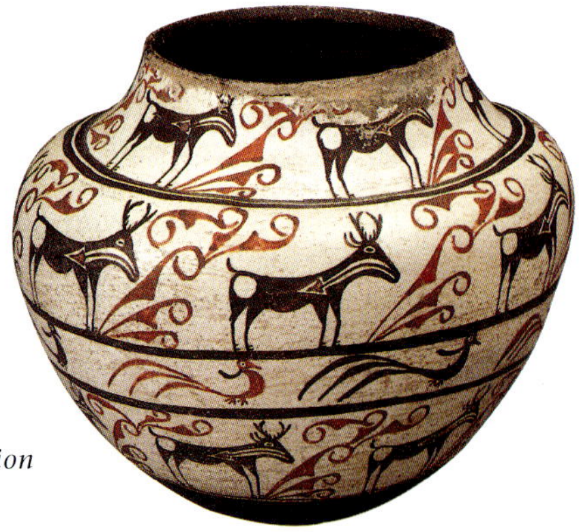

▶ 111

POLYCHROME JAR
ca. 1880
Height: 12½″

Collected by James Stevenson
Gift of the Women's Art Museum Association
through exchange with the United States
National Museum

1885.48

Selected Bibliography

Allen, Laura Graves
1984 *Contemporary Hopi Pottery*. Flagstaff: Museum of Northern Arizona.

Batkin, Jonathan
1987 *Pottery of the Pueblos of New Mexico, 1700-1940.* Colorado Springs: Taylor Museum of the Colorado Springs Fine Arts Center.

Babcock, Barbara and Doris Monthan
1986 *The Pueblo Storyteller.* Tucson: University of Arizona Press.

Bloom, Lansing
1933-1938 "Bourke on the Southwest." *New Mexico Historical Review.*

Brody, J. J.
1990 *Beauty from the Earth: Pueblo Indian Pottery from theUniversity Museum of Archaeology and Anthropology.* Philadelphia: University Museum of Archaeology and Anthropology.

The Anasazi. New York: Rizzoli.

Bunzel, Ruth L.
1929 *The Pueblo Potter: A Study of Creative Imagination in Primitive Art.* Columbia University Contributions to Anthropology 8. New York. Reprint. New York: Dover Publications, 1972.

Chapman, Kenneth M.
1936 *The Pottery of Santo Domingo Pueblo.* Laboratory of Anthropology Monograph 1. Reprint. Albuquerque: University of New Mexico Press, 1977.

1970 *The Pottery of San Ildefonso Pueblo.* School of American Research Monograph 28. Reprint. Albuquerque: University of New Mexico Press, 1977.

Dillingham, Rick
1994 *Fourteen Families in Pueblo Pottery.* Albuquerque: University of New Mexico Press.

Dillingham, Rick with Melinda Elliot
1992 *Acoma & Laguna Pottery.* Santa Fe: School of American Research Press.

Frank, Larry and Francis H. Harlow
1974 *Historic Pottery of the Pueblo Indians, 1600-1880.* Boston: New York Graphic Society.

Hardin, Margaret Ann
1983 *Gifts of Mother Earth: Ceramics in the Zuni Tradition.* Phoenix: Heard Museum.

LeFree, Betty
1975 *Santa Clara Pottery Today.* School of American Research Monograph 29. Albuquerque: University of New Mexico Press.

Maxwell Museum of Anthropology
1974 *Seven Families in Pueblo Pottery.* Reprint. Albuquerque: University of New Mexico Press, 1991.

Ortiz, Alfonso, ed.
1979 *Handbook of North American Indians, vol. 9, Southwest.* Washington, D.C.: Smithsonian Institution.

Peterson, Susan
1977 *The Living Tradition of Maria Martinez.* Tokyo: Kodansha International.

1984 *Lucy M. Lewis: American Indian Potter.* Tokyo: Kodansha International.

Rodee, Marion and James Ostler
1986 *Zuni Pottery.* West Chester Penn.: Schiffer Publishing.

Trimble, Stephen
1987 *Talking with the Clay: The Art of Pueblo Pottery.* Santa Fe: School of American Research Press.

Acknowledgments

A project such as the development of an exhibition and accompanying publication is not the result of only one person's efforts. It takes the support, dedication and cooperation of a great many people. In this endeavor I gladly acknowledge the generous support and encouragement of Roger Fry as the trustee of the August A. Rendigs, Jr. Foundation for this publication and The Lois and Richard Rosenthal Foundation for its sponsorship of the exhibition. Other longtime friends of the Museum who gave me their encouragement and support (as well as a place to stay on my collecting trips) were Bob and Lois Johannigman and Mary Courter.

I am also grateful for the generosity of those individuals who gifted the contemporary pottery to the Museum: Mr. and Mrs. J. Richard Andre, Gail and Fred Berger, Dabby Blatt, Angela Campbell, Mrs. Daniel S. Campbell, Myra and Louis Chabut, Mr. and Mrs. James J. Crowe, Dr. and Mrs. Sanford R. Courter, James Edgy and Robert Lee, Charles and Harriet Edwards, Stephanie Eha, Roger and Pat Fry, Robert and Lois Johannigman, Alex and Joan Keller, Bill and Pam Koenig, Manuel D. and Rhoda Mayerson, Gretchen B. McCormick, Cathy T. Mitchell, Norman A. Murdock, Susan and Clinton Nagy, Valerie L. Newell, Judge and Mrs. Mark A. Painter, Susan and Daniel Pfau, Daniel and Irene Randolph, Mr. and Mrs. Joseph H. Rohling, Julia R. Schiff, Lauren A. Schiff, Sarah C. Schiff, Thomas R. Schiff, Timothy A. Smith, Mr. and Mrs. Daniel Stricker, Carol and Theodore Striker, Mr. and Mrs. J. Dwight Thompson, Miss Hillary Thompson, Miss Megan Thompson, Mr. and Mrs. L. Harold Wehling.

Numerous staff members, past and present, have been instrumental in helping this project reach fruition. I am grateful to former Director Millard F. Rogers, Jr. and the Board of Directors for approving this project, and to the Museum's current director, Barbara Gibbs, for her continuing support. Acting Chief Curator Otto Thieme has been particularly helpful in his role as mentor. Cynthia Amneus, costume technician, also deserves special mention as does Gretchen McCormick, a devoted volunteer. The preparation of this publication would not have been possible without the patience and hard work of Ann Cotter, coordinator of Publications, and Joy Roe, coordinator of Photographic Services, and their assistant, Barbara King. Thanks also goes to Debbie Leffert for the design of this publication, Ron Forth, who photographed the pottery, and Katherine Juhl, for her comments on the manuscript. The design and installation of the exhibition were made possible through the efforts of Mary Ellen Goeke, head of Exhibitions and Registration; Patrick Brown, assistant chief preparator; Tim Rouch, intern; and the entire Exhibitions staff.

Several other people have also played key roles in helping to bring this project to life. Janice Klein, registrar at Field Museum of Natural History has always been willing to offer ideas and encouragement. My mother, Rowena Mercer, also deserves my special gratitude. She has always been incredibly supportive and I owe everything to her guidance. Our consultant, Mary Garcia, played a crucial role in this project. Her knowledge and pleasant nature made our trips a joy. Without her and the support of her family, none of this would have been possible. For their support and friendship I am most thankful.

I am especially grateful to the potters who so willingly opened their homes and their hearts when we arrived — often unannounced. I hope that in the exhibition and these pages we have done their talents justice. My deepest thanks are extended to: Autumn Borts, Linda Cain, Arthur and Hilda Coriz, Annette Duran, Ignacia Duran, Anthony Durand, Max Early, Fawn Garcia, Petra Garcia, Mary Lewis Garcia, Virginia Garcia, Katherine Gutierrez, Margaret Lou Gutierrez, Rita Donna Martinez, Lois Medina, Sofia Medina, Randy Nahohai, Louis and Virginia Naranjo, Virgil Ortiz, Brenda Paloma, Gabriel Paloma, Gladys Paquin, Anderson Peynetsa, Katherine Pino, Maria "Lilly" Salvador, Juan Tafoya, Lu Ann Tafoya, Mark Tahbo, Robert Tenorio, Elvis Torres, Albert and Josephine Vigil, and Priscilla Vigil.

It is to these talented individuals and all the other traditional Native American artists that this publication is dedicated.

Bill Mercer
Assistant Curator
Arts of Africa and the Americas